THE NATIONAL FREIGHT BUY-OUT

The inside story of how 10,000 people raised
£53.5 million to buy Britain's biggest freight
transport group from the Government.

THE NATIONAL FREIGHT BUY-OUT

Sandy McLachlan

Foreword by Peter Thompson

MACMILLAN PRESS
LONDON

First published 1983 by
THE MACMILLAN PRESS LTD
London and Basingstoke
Companies and representatives
throughout the world

ISBN 0 333 35370 6

Typeset in Great Britain by
Wessex Typesetters Ltd
Frome, Somerset
Printed in Great Britain by
Pitman Press
Bath

I am sure all NFC people would wish me to dedicate this book to the memory of Pat Thompson whose support of Peter Thompson contributed so much to his leadership of the Consortium.

CONTENTS

Government and Barclays Merchant Bank. Senior
managers are canvassed in secret, and are
enthusiastic.

x   *Contents*

FOREWORD

When we set out to buy the NFC from the Government we started with a very simple concept: 'Let us own the company we work for'. It proved to be much more difficult than any of us imagined and involved us deeply in the legal, financial, political and communications fields in ways which were sometimes pioneering. Lawyers, bankers, civil servants, accountants, politicians, PR men and above all NFC managers and their staffs became enthused with the concept. They were prepared to spend endless hours to bring success to our venture. Many wives hardly saw their husbands (and vice versa) for weeks on end. And at the end of it all over 10,000 NFC employees, pensioners and their families responded by putting down the money to buy control of this great business.

As a tribute to the people whose efforts made this possible, and to record a piece of industrial history, we felt we should commission this book. We hope that our example may be followed by others who seek new ways of getting rid of the 'us and them' – management versus workers – syndrome, which has dominated so much of British industry since the war.

It is time for new initiatives in the field of industrial ownership. It is time for new approaches and this book records one.

Sandy McLachlan has managed to capture the spirit as well as the detail of our story.

We hope you will find it as absorbing to read as we who were involved found it fascinating to play our parts in making it happen.

PETER THOMPSON
Chairman and Chief Executive
National Freight Consortium p.l.c.

xi

AUTHOR'S INTRODUCTION

When I was first approached to write this book my reaction was one of enthusiasm. Not only is the story of the NFC staff buy-out a fascinating one: it is also highly unusual for a financial journalist to be given free access to confidential company files *and* permission to publish the information contained in them. I am happy to say that my early enthusiasm was maintained.

Right at the outset National Freight Consortium p.l.c. promised its full co-operation and its backing to persuade other parties involved to co-operate. That was a brave promise to make – not least because the path to the end result of more than 80 per cent of NFC being owned by employees and pensioners of the company was seldom smooth and sometimes stormy. Moreover, the number of people involved from outside the NFC itself was considerable.

I hope that some of the detail contained in this book will bear testimony to the way that NFC fulfilled its promise. A lot of important and busy people were generous with their time in making this book possible. It would take too much space to list them individually – and inevitably it would be invidious, since I would be bound to leave somebody out. To all concerned, however, my grateful thanks.

Normally it is the financial journalist's lot to wait outside closed doors and receive an agreed statement from the parties concerned at the end of the day. It is then up to him to use his contacts to penetrate the barrier of bland phrases that has been strung together by an army of businessmen, accountants, lawyers, public relations consultants – and so on. Normally, too, he has varying degrees of success in finding out what really went on behind those closed doors.

In this case, virtually every door has been opened – albeit after the event, and what has emerged is not just the story of how the NFC deal was arranged and pushed through, but also an indication of how businesses really work in practice. Except in cases of complete disaster – when scapegoats are chosen and heads have to roll – decisions by managers, politicians, trade unionists, bankers and everyone else can be justified in retrospect. In reality, many decisions have to be based – at the time – on incomplete information: the secret of success is simply to be right more often than you are wrong.

The eventual success of NFC's removal from the public sector back to the private sector is clear proof that enough people got it right enough of the time. That is a considerable tribute to a group of people who were trying to break new ground while standing on a quicksand of uncertainty. To that extent I hope the book will be of interest not just to NFC employees and those who might wish to follow a similar route in the future – but also to a wider audience which is interested in how business decisions are made on the basis of knowledge, luck, foresight, experience, intuition, contacts – and – more luck.

Inevitably, some of the subjects covered in the following pages are highly technical: you can't do a – so far – unique deal with government to buy a £50 million-plus company of the complexity of NFC without running into all sorts of snags. As far as possible I have tried to keep the narrative in chronological order but interspersed throughout the book are chapters on complex subjects such as pension fund arrangements. For those not interested in such esoteric subjects, my advice is: skip those chapters!

The NFC management commissioned this book to tell shareholders, other staff, and anyone else who is interested, just how the buy-out was accomplished. They are proud of their achievement – and, in my view, rightly so.

April 1983   *Sandy McLachlan*

1

THE BACKGROUND

The National Freight Consortium is the product of a long line of decisions by politicians, railwaymen, businessmen, and ordinary people.

> First sentence of a paper delivered by Philip Mayo, Director of Legal Services, National Freight Consortium p.l.c., to Industrial Society conference, June 17, 1982.

That statement is a succinct account of what this book is about. But behind those 20 words lies a fascinating story with the, sometimes nail-biting, truth every bit as exciting as fiction could be.

It is the story of how the ownership of a British nationalised undertaking, the National Freight Corporation, passed from the hands of the Government of the day to the people who work in the National Freight Consortium p.l.c. (as it now is), their immediate kin, and NFC pensioners.

In fact, it is a story of many stories. It has the spice of politics and politicians at the highest level; money to the tune of over £50 million; banks in the City; trades unions and management. Above all, however, it is a story about people.

Approximately 10,300 people used savings and/or loans to raise £6,187,500 to buy their own company: indeed they did better than that, the offer of shares was oversubscribed by

£800,000 and share applications had to be scaled down accordingly.

The sums of money subscribed are less important than the number of people: the 10,000-plus figure means that about a quarter of the employees and pensioners eligible to buy shares did so.

That may not sound startling, but the majority of NFC employees – many of them drivers, mechanics and clerical staff – would never before have considered even the remote possibility of buying shares. Such savings as they had would more likely be in a Post Office Savings account or in a building society. A very high proportion of the 10,300 have become shareholders in British industry for the first time: that in itself is remarkable, given that the trend over the period since the war has been for the number of private shareholders to decline and more and more of shares in public companies to be concentrated in the hands of institutions such as pension funds and insurance companies.

Their reasons and their views are treated in some depth later in the book, but the fact that they backed management proposals has given the story a happy ending. Thanks to management initiative, an imaginative communications programme, a degree of union acceptance, and the wholehearted support of a relatively new London merchant bank, those 10,000-plus people now control between them 82.5 per cent of the company they work for or are associated with. Because of this staff-related support, Barclays Merchant Bank (BMB) was able to put together a package that allowed the management-led consortium to buy National Freight Company Ltd from the Government at a price of £53.5 million. BMB achieved this by putting together a group of most of the leading clearing banks, including its own parent, that took up the remaining 17.5 per cent of the equity in the group. In return the banks agreed to lend the Consortium £51 million on a medium term basis, to provide £30 million of overdraft facility to give the company working capital, and BMB agreed to provide NFC p.l.c. with up to £3 million for it to set up an employee loan scheme to help its staff to invest in their own company.

The eventual success of this package – whose progress was fraught with, sometimes almost insuperable, difficulties makes NFC a unique animal. It is a major public limited company with no share quotation on the London Stock Exchange, although shareholders will have the right to opt for a full quotation after five years if they so wish. With over 10,000 people holding shares the exercise could hardly be described as a management buy-out, but nor does NFC bear any resemblance to a workers' co-operative: it is a properly constituted public company, governed by its Articles of Association, and owned by its shareholders who have the right to appoint or remove directors in the same way that applies to any other public company. The uniqueness of the eventual deal stems from several factors: its size makes it the biggest buy-out so far by a long chalk; the vast majority of shareholders are employees, their families, former employees and pensioners, and it took a change in company law to make the final deal possible in its present form.

Even so it would be wrong to be too euphoric about the outcome. It has proved a great success for the new shareholders, but that has as much to do with outside factors such as falling interest rates – which always work in favour of a company that has a very high debt to equity ratio – as it has with successful management.

It is not necessarily a good thing for workers to own their own company: it is dangerous for people to put all their eggs in one basket since, if anything did go wrong with the company, those people who invested in it would lose not just their jobs, but at least part of their savings as well. But, to be fair to management in NFC's case, although considerable employee support was needed to make the deal possible, workers were advised not to over-commit themselves. Also, the team that set up the deal were able to convince hard-headed bankers that it was a good idea to the tune of over £50 million.

As the tale unfolds it will become clear that there were other alternatives to be taken into consideration. Once this nationalised undertaking had been converted into a limited liability company it was the Government's intention to sell all, or at least a majority, of the shares to the general public. This would have involved an Offer for Sale, to use stock market parlance, and, with NFC's somewhat chequered profit performance in the past few years, the sale price would not have come anywhere near the value put on the assets owned by NFC. Moreover, the advice of one of London's top merchant banks – J. Henry Schroder Wagg – was that, with a weakening market, it was not a good time to sell. One of the implications of this was that the newly 'privatised' company would be ripe for a takeover bid by a company more interested in making a profit by selling off the assets than keeping NFC as a going concern. Many a fortune has been founded on asset-stripping.

As the management of NFC saw it at the time, there was also the distinct possibility that the Conservative Government itself might be forced to indulge in a little asset-stripping. Committed in its 1979 election manifesto to divest itself of the NFC, and faced with the near-impossibility of a straightforward Offer for Sale, the Government might have been forced to sell the group off piecemeal. This would have resulted in the most profitable parts of the organisation being sold off bit by bit to other companies, while the less profitable and loss-making subsidiaries would have been left in public ownership – with the prospect of eventual closedown. Another alternative would have been for the Government to sell the whole of NFC to a single purchaser. The NFC feared that this could introduce an alien management style and a large amount of rationalisation. In either event little or no benefit would have been likely to accrue to the workers of NFC, and almost inevitably a number of them would have gone to swell further the already swollen ranks of the unemployed.

No staff buy-out of this magnitude had ever been achieved before, but the Consortium proved that it is possible for management to communicate with a large, geographically widespread, and, in the main, financially unsophisticated workforce to the extent that a high proportion of this workforce now accepts that everyone is working towards the same goals.

Too many people glibly put down the German 'economic miracle' as being the result of its losing the Second World War, and it is true that the country got a head start with a reconstruction based on plant and equipment. But one of the main reasons for the sustained success of German industry is that 'both sides' of industry have been on the same side: workers' representatives badger management for improved productivity, because they know that real wealth is created that way. So far that has been an element sadly lacking on the British industrial scene; now, in the case of NFC, many of its workers know that they have a direct financial stake in the success of their own group. Union support for the deal may have been lukewarm (and one union, the Transport and General Workers, was implacably opposed to the idea), but there is considerable evidence that privatisation by the NFC route has produced much better communication between grass roots and top management.

But to understand the events of the past three years that have brought about this situation, it is necessary to consider the background that led to the rather curious nature of the NFC animal that the 1979 Conservative Government wanted to sell back to the private sector. For that one must go back to 1948 when the post-war Labour Government was busy implementing its manifesto promises to bring large sections of the economy into public ownership.

In that year the Government set up the British Transport Commission, which subsequently acquired the thousands of firms and companies engaged in long distance freight transport in the United Kingdom. The railway companies, too, were nationalised at that time, bringing their substantial road haulage interests into the public sector as well as the actual rail network itself.

In the ping-pong fashion that has resulted from the diam-
etrically opposing views on state intervention of the two main
political parties since the war, the Conservative Party began to
dismantle this transport leviathan in 1953. The majority of
road haulage operations were sold back to the private sector –
either to their original owners or to other private interests. Not
all the road haulage activities were divested, however, and
those that remained were grouped under the British Road
Services banner, while British Railways continuted to operate
its own road transport interests.

Although there have been many subsequent changes, there
has been no attempt at a full-scale renationalisation of
long-distance road haulage, and that has meant that the
state-owned road haulage interests have been in an anomalous
position. It is normal for a nationalised industry to enjoy a
monopoly position in its field and, since the unwinding of the
British Transport Commission, that has certainly not been the
case in road haulage. The industry is an extremely fragmented
one, with no single operator having a large share and only one
having around 7 per cent of the commercial road haulage
market, and that single operator is NFC. Commercial road
haulage excludes in-house ('own-account') fleets operated by
manufacturers or traders. These apart, the typical road
haulage operator is small, running no more than five vehicles.

Therefore, state-owned road transport activities have found
themselves governed by nationalised industry rules, but competing for business in a very open market – often against small,
low-overhead, operators in each geographical area. With
market conditions varying in different parts of the country,
there also needs to be a considerable amount of management
autonomy at area, and even local, levels.

After 1953, the next major move was in 1962 when an
attempt was made to rationalise all the government-owned
(non-rail) transport activities. A Transport Holding Company
(THC) was set up which brought in Thomas Cook, the
companies which were to form a large part of what is now the

National Bus Company, and several shipping lines as well, to add to the road freight interests. As far as the road freight activities were concerned, the main importance of that Act was that it enabled the THC to acquire further businesses by negotiation, and several were acquired in this way.

But for the National Freight Corporation, the key legislation was the 1968 Transport Act – not least because it was this Act which brought the NFC into existence with roughly its present operating subsidiaries. The bus companies went to form the National Bus Company, and Thomas Cook was left with the Transport Holding Company, but the newly formed NFC took over the road haulage operations which previously had been operated by the railways.

The political aim of the 1968 Act was to integrate freight services throughout the country, but with a specific proviso that as much freight as possible should be channelled by rail. Indeed one of the NFC companies – Freightliners – was jointly owned with the railways. But, ironically, it was the provisions of the 1968 Act setting up the NFC that – over 10 years later – were to pose some of the trickiest problems in returning road freight activities to the private sector.

For a start, from an NFC point of view, the deal would never have been done for commercial reasons: the Sundries Division of British Railways – renamed National Carriers – was at that time in the late sixties, to quote one source, 'massively unprofitable and overmanned'. In 1968 it achieved a loss of over £20 million on a turnover of £25 million. Moreover, of the 66,000 staff employed by NFC when it was set up, no less than 25,000 were ex-railwaymen or, to be more accurate, more or less ex-railwaymen. Under the terms of the Act they were guaranteed that transfer to NFC would make them no worse off than they had been under the auspices of BR, and that meant that they retained travel concessions and, much more important for the future in terms of problems, stayed in railway pension funds.

The government of the day recognised that it was burdening

*The largest constituent companies
of the NFC carry well-known
names. Activities range from the
transport, storage and distribution
of freight to waste management, car
transport, travel and wine shipping.*

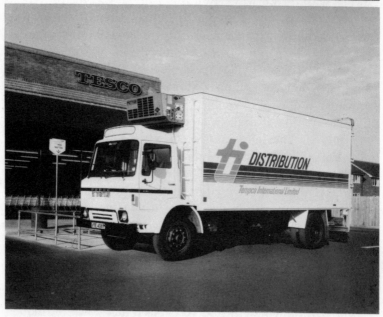

the new NFC with considerable losses as a result of the transfer of the BR activities and acknowledged this by giving the Corporation subsidies in the early years. These subsidies were phased out by 1973 (earlier than planned) since good trading conditions plus a considerable reduction in the burden of excess manpower and vehicles brought the Corporation into profit. But the structure of the NFC and the activities in which it was allowed to participate were still governed by the fairly rigid terms of the 1968 Act.

Jumping ahead, NFC did well within these constraints. Between the 1968 Act and 1979 the workforce had been cut from 66,000 people to 34,500 and the number of vehicles from 29,000 to 18,500; by the time that the buy-out was under consideration the workforce was down to around 28,000 and the number of vehicles to around 16,000, and all this was achieved without any significant industrial relations problems.

But that is not to say that there were not considerable problems in other areas. Following the 1968 Act the NFC improved its trading position steadily, and made small trading profits between 1972–74. However the recession of 1975 hit the group hard and it made a sizeable trading loss, which grew to £31 million after interest and exceptional items (mostly concerned with foreign investments) were taken into account. This led the Government to put in financial consultants, and subsequently to provide financial support accompanied by severe restraints, for example on investment.

In 1976 virtually the whole of the top management team was changed, beginning with the appointment of Mr Peter Thompson as Chief Executive (Operations), and the majority of the new team had outside industrial or financial experience prior to joining NFC. They carried on with the policy of trying to insulate the group from economic cycles by running down the general and unprofitable sides of the freight business, and concentrating on specialised services which were more profitable and less vulnerable.

However, the group was still burdened with an enormous

capital debt to the Government, which involved heavy interest payments. Some help was given by a Labour government in 1978 when NFC underwent a capital reconstruction. The Government wrote off £53 million of NFC's capital debt – although this still left NFC with £100 million to service with interest – and the Corporation got a £15 million grant for capital expenditure as well as relief from some pension and travel obligations it had inherited from BR with National Carriers.

With some help from these measures, group trading profit increased steadily up until 1978 to a peak of £20.8 million. But there were two other problems outstanding. One was a substantial deficiency on the various pension funds which would have to be funded at some stage, and the other was government pay policy in the public sector which, when implemented, applied to nationalised industries as well. Over the years that had created considerable discrepancies between the salaries of top management in the public and private sectors, and also introduced rigidities into pay bargaining.

That last difficulty was one that denationalisation could solve, but the rest of the group's problems were to pose the question: just how could the NFC be denationalised? Although it contained household names such as Pickfords, it also carried the problem of National Carriers. It had an improving, though patchy, profit performance at the trading level, but an enormous burden of debt and considerable pension liabilities. It was expanding into new areas such as cold storage, but moves in such directions were hampered by the restrictions of the 1968 Transport Act.

The answer to that question took three years and an incalculable number of man-hours – certainly running into hundreds of thousands – to find. That answer, when it came, was a unique solution: that is what this book is all about.

2

THE EARLY DAYS

Our preferred solution . . . is to seek private investment in the NFC, and provide a corporation similar (although not necessarily identical) in make-up to British Petroleum.

> Extract from the 1977 Conservative Party Document On Transport Policy, 'The Right Track', by the then Shadow Transport Minister, Norman Fowler.

On March 16 1979 – General Election year – the *Daily Telegraph* published an article by one of its most respected business correspondents, Roland Gribben. The first two paragraphs read as follows:

A wide-ranging shake-up involving denationalisation, hiving off parts of other state corporations and substantial cuts in the £2,500 million a year subsidies will form part of a Conservative Government's industrial policy.

The National Freight Corporation is understood to be one of the candidates earmarked for selling to the private sector. Some other smaller state industries would be reduced to a 'British Petroleum' status, with the Government stake cut to 51 per cent.

That article caused considerable consternation at the Argosy House, London, headquarters of NFC. The same day, Brian Cottee, Head of Communication Services for the Corporation, spoke to Mr Gribben who, while naturally declining to name his source for the article, intimated that it was, in his view, totally reliable. Before the day was out Mr Cottee had circulated an internal memorandum to the Board and the executive committee which said, *inter alia*: 'Should we not take steps to impress on all possible Tory sources the unsaleability of the NFC as an entity, and the "rump" problems of piecemeal sales?' The hare was off and running on what was to prove to be a somewhat erratic course.

Brian Cottee recalls that the immediate concern at the time was the effect on employees and customers of speculation about a sell-off which might never be pursued, or which might become a piecemeal disposal of the profitable parts, when the full extent of the NFC's liabilities and problems became known.

The implications of the 1977 Conservative Party Policy document on transport 'The Right Track', had not been lost on NFC management, but the article in the *Daily Telegraph* was the first indication that transport specifically might be a major plank in the forthcoming Conservative Manifesto. The people running NFC were quietly pleased with the progress that was being made to rationalise and improve the trading potential of a group that had been put together on political rather than on financial or industrial logic, but were under no illusions about its lack of attractiveness in stock market terms. This emerged very early on in the piece, in a five-page memorandum from corporate planning director Gerry Flanagan which was produced within a week of the newspaper article.

The memorandum, which initially was circulated only to the chairman, three other directors, and the chief executive, looked at the various possibilities open for denationalising NFC, and discounted a sell-off:

The first and obvious problem for a Secretary of State in

implementing that. . . would be the need to find a purchaser. It is difficult to imagine a single purchaser being terribly interested. Since the NFC is itself a conglomerate the managerial problems for another conglomerate taking us over would be formidable. It seems equally unlikely that there would be any great rush to buy shares if we were simply floated on the market – at least at any but knockdown prices, which would produce political objections that the Nation's assets were being given away to the Government's friends. It is also hard to see how a policy of outright sale of the entire Corporation could be compatible with the over-riding need of any Government to achieve some kind of *modus vivendi* with the trade unions.

This posed a problem.

At this stage the directors and the executive committee of NFC were punching at a bag of cotton wool: the election manifestos of the parties had not been published and the outcome of the election was by no means a foregone conclusion. Undoubtedly, through the political contacts of some of the Board members, NFC had some inkling of what the manifestos would say in relation to the Corporation. Indeed one non-executive director, Frank Law, wrote to Mrs Thatcher pointing out the damage that uncertainty was producing. He was put in touch with Norman Fowler and later an important friendship was to develop between the two men. But that apart, the group executives were trying to formulate contingency plans in a vacuum. Although nothing appears about it in the files for another month, it is clear from conversations with members of the then executive committee that the idea of a 'BP solution' was not unattractive even at that stage: with BP, the government sold off 49 per cent of the company to institutions and the general public and retained a controlling 51 per cent stake – but at the same time gave assurances that it would not interfere with the commercial running of the company. At NFC this option, first mentioned by Norman Fowler in 1977 had, potentially at least, certain distinct advantages. Details, such as the effect on the Corporation's ability to borrow from the government, would have to be sorted out, but at least NFC would be freed from the shackles of nationalised industry status. The prospect of being allowed to operate on a wholly commercial basis – whoever owned the company, or shares in the company – was attractive to a top management most of whom had spent the formative part of their working lives in the private sector. It was only much later that it transpired that this was a red herring – in the sense that the Conservatives had changed their thinking since 1977, and never seriously considered a BP solution for NFC, particularly since the Group's unusual pension problems rendered it a financial non-starter.

Early in April 1979 the party manifestos were published. The Liberal Party walked down the white line in the middle of the road as far as state-ownership was concerned: 'There is no case for further large-scale nationalisation in Britain; but attempts to denationalise at present would further disrupt the industries affected'.

Predictably, Labour drove on the left on transport policies: 'The National Freight Corporation must be enabled to provide the basis for expanding the public sector in the road haulage industry.' That brief quote represents an example of the Labour Party's determination to revive large-scale nationalisation as a cure for the country's economic ills – with transport one of the priorities.

But, at the end of the day, only one manifesto was to count and that was the Conservatives'. On nationalisation it had this to say:

The British people strongly oppose Labour's plans to nationalise yet more firms and industries such as building, banking, insurance, pharmaceuticals and road haulage. More nationalisation would further impoverish us and further undermine our freedom. We will offer to sell back to private ownership the recently nationalised aerospace and shipbuilding concerns, giving their employees the opportunity to purchase shares.

More specifically on road transport it said:

> We aim to sell shares in the National Freight Corporation to the general public in order to achieve substantial private investment in it.

On the first Thursday in May 1979 a Conservative Government was to be swept back to power on this platform with a comfortable majority. But in the three weeks before the election NFC management had taken note of the glaringly obvious: National Freight Corporation was the only group in the public sector to be identified in the Tory manifesto as a target for denationalisation or, to use that unpleasant modern word, privatisation.

Ironically, given the potential conflict between road and rail in freight transport, the same chapter in the Tory manifesto referred to British Rail. It said:

> High productivity is the key to the future of industries like British Rail, where improvement would benefit both the workforce and passengers who have faced unprecedented fare increases over the last five years.

Much later in the piece this seemingly innocuous paragraph was to cause NFC considerable embarrassment at a crucial time in the Corporation's plans, and rationalisation at BR was to cost the Corporation dear. A joint venture on which the Corporation was making money and BR was losing money was scrapped – downgrading profit forecasts for NFC at almost exactly the wrong moment.

But NFC was quick to react to the Tory manifesto as it applied directly to its own affairs. The day after the manifesto was published – on April 12 1979 – the Corporation issued a

somewhat Delphic statement to its workforce. It read as
follows:

> The specific references to the NFC in the manifesto represent
> a vote of confidence in the Corporation, and recognise its
> value to industry. It has always been the NFC's policy to look
> for opportunities to expand selectively into activities where
> business prospects are good, though lack of cash has limited
> its actual expansion.
>
> The Corporation has often suggested that it would benefit
> from more flexible financing. At present the NFC's capital is
> in the form of loans on which it is obliged to pay interest every
> year at rates set by Government.
>
> However, the ownership of the shares is not a matter for
> us, but for Parliament. Whatever is decided, the vital issue
> for the NFC as a public enterprise in a competitive market is
> to ensure an efficient Corporation giving a good return on the
> assets which Parliament has placed in its care.

Obviously a lot of thought went into that statement, because
what it really says is: yes we would like a BP-type solution but,
no, we are not getting dragged into the mill of politics. (The
election was still some weeks ahead.) Indeed, throughout the
entire exercise of divorcing itself from government control the
NFC did its best to talk in strictly commercial terms, although
the eventual solution of a staff buy-out had, inevitably, strong
political overtones.

At this stage, however, the idea of a buy-out had not entered
anyone's head: but some of the possible implications involved
in unwinding the Corporation were giving senior management
considerable cause for concern. Some of these (publicly
unspoken) fears were given an independent airing in the Lex
column of the *Financial Times* on April 26 1979: the article
pointed out that, on past performance of the NFC, a Tory
Government might have to wait a few years before it could float
NFC on the stock market; it referred to the Corporation's

'spotty' profit record, and suggested that a capital reconstruction would be necessary before anything at all could be done. This prophetic argument concluded:

> If the Tories wanted quicker action, however, they could sell bits of NFC off to private sector companies. Such a move would be very unpopular with management, but there certainly are parts of the business which could be sold tomorrow if such a course were considered acceptable.

That solution – as Lex pointed out – was the last thing that NFC management wanted, since it would mean an asset stripping venture on a governmental scale: profitable enterprises such as Pickfords would be hived off, leaving NFC with Mr Cottee's 'rump' of unprofitable businesses in the public sector.

While Lex was making its assessment, NFC was doing some sums of its own. On April 27 1979 a Board paper was produced entitled 'The Effect on NFC of a Conservative Government'. It did not come before the Board until May 8 – by which time the Conservative Government had been elected with a comfortable majority – but it was the first serious attempt to analyse the options available to a new government, and to put a possible price tag on the National Freight Corporation.

Rejoicing in the anonymity of being 'Board Paper NF 1241' and coming in front of members at the Corporation's 120th Board Meeting, the paper singled out three options which were considered to be 'the most obvious and practical'. The first was a straight Offer for Sale as a Companies Act company, the second an Offer for Sale of NFC minus its main loss-makers, and the third piecemeal sales of NFC companies which had a track record sufficient to make them attractive to the stock market. That paper also made two crucial assumptions: one was that NFC would be turned into a normal company as opposed to being a nationalised corporation, and the other was that the pension fund deficiencies 'could somehow be funded'.

All in all, that particular Board Paper did not make happy reading. The third option – piecemeal sales of profitable divisions – was rejected as being unacceptable to both a Tory administration and to the Corporation. Option 2 – selling NFC as a package minus its main loss-makers National Carriers and Roadline – was damned with faint praise: on one hand 'it is the only one which offers any prospect of meeting the manifesto pledge in the immediate future.' On the other : 'Managerial and operational complexities involved might well . . . take so much time and effort to resolve as to rob the idea of its attraction'.

That, therefore, left option 1, which in many ways was no more attractive than the discarded alternatives. To quote the Paper again:

> for NFHL (National Freight Holdings Ltd) to 'go public' on the basis of the 1978 or prospective 1979 figures would mean making the offer at a price which would represent a very substantial discount on book value. . . . A valuation based on the projected 1980 results (assuming they are achieved) would be reasonably close to net asset values. But a prospectus based on audited 1980 results could not be issued before mid-1981. So the practicality of this option depends on the acceptability, to both the Secretary of State and the Board, of this (or a longer) timescale.

Although this Paper was prepared even before the election it clarifies two of the main issues wonderfully: pricing and timing. That original Board Paper estimated the 1980 value of the company in stock market terms to be between £61 million (based on earnings) and £93 million (based on potential dividend yield). True, it stated that the lower figure was 'more appropriate', but even that turned out to be over-optimistic. When the Board considered this paper at its May 8 meeting, the minutes state: 'the view was expressed that certain of the financial assumptions reflected in the supporting appendices were too optimistic and should be re-examined'. The parents of the buy-out idea were the down-grading of NFC's value and the ever-extending timetable for a conventional Offer for Sale through the stock market.

With a Conservative Government elected, one uncertainty was removed from the picture, but it was still a confusing time for NFC's top management: the Tory manifesto specifically mentioned the Corporation, but in the Queen's Speech on May 15 1979, there were simply proposals to 'reduce the extent of nationalised and State ownership and increase competition by providing offers for sale, including opportunities for employees to participate where appropriate'. There was no specific mention of NFC in the legislative programme.

At that stage even the specific mention of employee participation did not spark any thoughts of a staff buy-out in the minds of NFC's senior management, but they had reached the conclusion that outside financial advice would be – to say the least – helpful. Even before the Queen was outlining the policies that her new Government was to pursue, the NFC was sounding out leading merchant bankers. The Corporation talked seriously to just two – and decided that J. Henry Schroder Wagg & Co. (Schroders) was the right bank for NFC.

Schroders is one of London's – and therefore the world's – top merchant banks and its advice over both pricing and timing for a public offer did not favour early flotation. Minds started ticking over about alternative solutions, and time was to prove that it was not the right bank to provide the backing ultimately sought by the management for its buy-out.

The banks earn themselves a chapter elsewhere in this book, but Schroders' reaction is crucial to the narrative. In a nutshell, Schroders initially came up with a valuation that could have been anywhere between £57 million and £90 million on the open market – depending on the assumptions that were made on required yields and price/earnings ratios. This assessment was produced in July 1979, and was based on a timetable of coming to the market by mid-1981 at the earliest.

Schroders entered two caveats:

(a) the performance of the NFC in the meantime does not differ significantly from the forecasts provided and no material change occurs relevant to the prospects thereafter; and

(b) there is no significant change in stock market conditions compared with the present.

In the event neither of these conditions was to be met. The recession was to force·a downgrading of NFC forecasts and an equally important change in stock market sentiment. Schroders' views on both price and timing were to become increasingly cautious – pushing the launch date into 1982 and possibly 1983 and bringing the price tag on the Corporation down to around £50 million. In fact the bank had been quite specific about its preferred timetable in the original document:

Had the NFC been a privately-owned company whose shareholders had been seeking our advice regarding the timing of a possible offer for sale to the public, we would have favoured a later date than proposed, probably 1982 or 1983. This would have enabled a longer record of profits to be shown and the benefits of business developments and reorganisation to have been demonstrated.

At this early stage Schroders made three telling points. The first was that NFC would have to be a Companies Act company if it were to be floated off to the public, either in whole or in part, and the other two points followed from this: the bank took the view that the fixed interest debt to government should be made into risk-bearing equity capital, and that a Stock Exchange quotation would not be feasible unless the pension fund deficit were properly funded.

The summer and autumn of 1979 proved to be a difficult time for all concerned. On June 21 Norman Fowler answered a

Parliamentary Question: 'I am actively considering ways and means of putting into effect the Conservative Manifesto promise to achieve a substantial element of private investment in the NFC'. *Hansard* records his answer to a supplementary question put by Tory MP Peter Viggers: 'My preferred approach is to retain the NFC in the form in which it is broadly constituted at present. I would prefer to see private investment in the NFC'.

But hours, weeks and even months were slipping away. Although the NFC was specifically mentioned in the pre-election Tory manifesto, the new Government was also, subsequently, committed to privatise British Aerospace, part of the British National Oil Corporation (now BritOil), British Airways and British Shipbuilders. To achieve this, thousands of millions of pounds would have to be found from the private sector, and although the capital markets in the UK are arguably the most efficient in the world, the amount of private sector money available at any one time is limited: the private side of the UK economy may make money – but, unlike government, it cannot print it.

When companies outside the public sector are trying to raise new capital 'the queue' to tap the market for funds is organised by the Bank of England, whose job it is to ensure an orderly market. When the government wants to raise money from the private sector – either by borrowing or selling off state controlled assets – the procedure is much the same except in that case the Bank 'advises' rather than dictates.

Such considerations may appear remote to people driving, servicing, or organising the movement of freight vehicles: the City of London tends to be a closed book to those who do not work there. But the impact of 'City' factors, allied to political considerations, played a big part in the final outcome.

On the political side there were other problems to be faced. The Transport Bill which would enable the Secretary of State to sell off NFC was not published until November 17 1979. It did not have an easy passage through all the stages that proposed legislation has to pass before it becomes law, and it was not until June 1980 that the Bill received Royal Assent – thus making it Law. Even then it was only enabling legislation; it *allowed* the Minister of Transport (Norman Fowler) to create the conditions that would transform a state-controlled corporation into a limited company, and *allowed* him the right to sell shares in this new company as he saw fit. It did not *compel* him to do anything at all.

Already however, officials at the Department of Transport were anticipating the likely wishes of their political masters and were pleasantly surprised to discover how much homework NFC had already done. The main points that were to emerge in the Act had already been established a year earlier following discussions between NFC, the Department of Transport, Schroders and the Treasury.

On the 'Appointed Day' mentioned in the Act, but the timing left to the Minister, NFC would become a Companies Act company, with its debt to the Minister (£100 million) extinguished, and, in exchange, leaving him owning the equity in the company. It was also accepted that the Government would fund pension-fund liabilities on an actuarial basis. (At that time the deficit was thought to be around £40 million: in the end it turned out to be £8 million greater.)

For NFC the Act was merely a step along the road towards achieving private investment, and had no real significance until such time as the Secretary of State 'appointed the day' when the reconstruction of the Corporation into National Freight Company Ltd should take place.

There was quite a battle over the timing of this event. Peter Thompson and his executive team, with the help of Schroders, pushed aggressively for an immediate change of status, the main point of their argument being that the longer NFC had a track record as a company before coming to the stock market, the better were the chances of the market accepting a favourable valuation of the company. Mr Thompson was anxious to demonstrate the improved quality of NFC management, plans and planning, under the rules prevailing in the private sector: in his and his colleagues' view NFC had never been a nationalised industry in the accepted sense of the word because of its lack of monopoly position, and the sooner that this and the structural changes in the way the business was run which had taken place in the preceding few years were recognised – the better for all concerned.

Ranged against this approach was the formidable opposition of the Treasury. The way in which that august Department watches the governmental purse strings in the most parsimonious fashion possible is legendary, and the moment that the capital structure was changed from loan to equity finance, the Government stood to lose interest payments totalling millions of pounds a year. Not surprisingly, the Treasury wanted the 'Appointed Day' to be as close as possible to public flotation in order to retain maximum interest payments from NFC.

Peter Thompson's team won this particular battle: National Freight Company Ltd took over the assets and liabilities of National Freight Corporation on October 1 1980 – well before there was any chance of bringing NFC to the market. In the meantime, Schroders was beginning to find its role as financial advisers to both NFC and the Government (it had agreed to act for both parties at the Government's request in autumn 1979) more and more taxing.

Schroders did not find this an easy role to assume. In the first place, to quote one of the bank's directors, 'we agonised over the dual role since there were bound to be points of difference between the two sides'. Secondly, the storm clouds were gathering in terms of the recession; according to the same director: 'as time went on we became increasingly nervous about NFC's results'.

Other factors too were beginning to come into the equation. It was clear to all that British Aerospace was to be the first venture to be sold off by the Government (this happened, successfully, in January 1981), and there were fears expressed by NFC management that this might cause political pressure to be brought to bear on Norman Fowler to get on with selling NFC – even if it meant an alternative solution to a stock market offering. Unbeknown to NFC, the Department of Transport was looking around for a possible single purchaser for the whole business. However, NFC management had guessed this intention and was discussing internally who might or might not be acceptable to them. What NFC could not know was that its biggest single fear – a break-up of the group – was never seriously considered by the Government, for the reason that had been highlighted 18 months previously: the Government would have been left with the unprofitable bits.

In September 1980, in the very week that the Secretary of State sanctioned the change from Corporation to Company, NFC suffered another body-blow which was to seal the fate of any prospect of a 1981 flotation. British Rail, under considerable pressure to halt its own mounting losses, had decided that one easy area to cut back would be on its Express Parcels Service (BREPS) and in September 1980 Norman Fowler agreed with Peter Parker to make the finance available to do this. This was a joint venture with NFC, which handled the road collection and delivery side, and by a quirk in pricing policies not uncommon within nationalised industries it was causing heavy losses for BR, but represented a substantial volume of profitable turnover for NFC. When the arrangement was wound up BR contributed towards NFC's run-down costs (most of the staff involved were ex-railway employees anyway), but left the Company with a substantial tab to pick up.

All the time, therefore, price and timing considerations were moving against NFC, and its senior executives were becoming irritated as well as concerned at developments. The group had been on a recovery tack since 1976, and management felt that the real gains achieved through rationalisation and diversification into more profitable new businesses should not be overshadowed by the fact that the crucial 1980 profit figures would be depressed by factors well beyond their control. Gradually an unspoken conviction was forming that NFC was in danger of being sold down the river, and as that conviction grew it became translated into an entirely new potential solution that might please the Government and be highly satisfactory from the NFC's own point of view. The thought was:

> We know this is well on the way to being a good business – we know what we have done to make it so. This action has yet to come through in the trading figures and we still worry that a predator will buy us – so why not buy ourselves?

3

THE BUY-OUT IS BORN

In early 1981 then, a group of senior managers began to
consider whether the management themselves might mount
a bid to acquire the company for themselves and for their
fellow employees.

> Extract from a speech by Philip Mayo,
> Director of Legal Services for NFC; June
> 1982.

It is hard to pinpoint, in any situation, when a vague concept
becomes a real possibility. In the case of NFC it is more difficult
than usual because when the process took place external
circumstances were changing, and so too was the NFC's own
internal structure. Particularly at the top the roles of individuals were undergoing a significant transformation.

In the crucial early period – in 1979 – the 'Board' of the
National Freight Corporation was composed of a powerful and
influential team from industry, commerce and the academic
world.* But, with the exception of Victor Paige, they were all

---

* Mr R. L. E. Lawrence, Mr J. S. Flemming, Mr F. S. Law, Mr D. G.
MacDonald, Mr V. G. Paige, Mr J. E. B. Sieve, Sir Ronald Swayne, Mr P. H.

non-executives – and Mr Paige was to become a part-time executive and deputy chairman at the end of 1979 when he was appointed chairman of the Port of London Authority.

The running of the Corporation was in the hands of an executive committee headed by Peter Thompson. He had resigned from the Board in 1978 on purely financial considerations: as a Board member of a nationalised industry his salary had been frozen for two years. On his own admission, Mr Thompson had considered quitting NFC altogether, but the Board persuaded him to stay as chief executive of the group and, although no longer a Board member, he did attend all Board meetings.

This type of managerial structure is not uncommon in banks and building societies, but it is a rare bird indeed in industrial organisations. In the case of NFC it created a distance between the guiding hand of the 'Board' (formally, 'the Members of the Corporation' – another oddity of organisation) and the executive committee which ran the business day to day. When the idea of a management buy-out – which became a management-led staff buy-out – was hatched by the executive team it was thus at arm's length from the Board. In the event, however, by the time the buy-out proposal was put to the Board in March 1981 the National Freight Company Ltd had superseded the Corporation (on October 1) and by that time the Board was predominantly an executive one,* including

---

Spriddell. Mr Lawrence was a vice-chairman of British Rail; Mr Flemming was investment bursar at Nuffield College, Oxford; Mr Law was chairman of the Varta Group, the Altana Group and the IWKA Group; Mr MacDonald was managing director of John Menzies (Holdings); Mr Paige was NFC deputy chairman; Mr Sieve was a director of Metal Box; Sir Ronald Swayne was chairman of OCL and the Australia Japan Container Line; and Mr Spriddell was a director of Marks and Spencer.

* From September 17 1980 the Board comprised Sir Robert Lawrence (Chairman), Mr V. G. Paige (deputy chairman), Mr P. A. Thompson†

three prime protagonists of the buy-out (Messrs Thompson, Mather and Watson) and two others who subsequently participated as members of the buy-out organising committee – Messrs Hayward and White.

Nevertheless, as the buy-out proposals took shape and developed, the Board had to remain alert to its legal obligation to safeguard the public interest: the public owned the business. While it was still, with its official financial adviser, concentrating on the Government's preferred aim of an Offer for Sale to the general public there could be no cause for conflict until the buy-out solution was officially mooted, and later, when the buy-out scheme was tabled, any possible division of interest was avoided by the way in which the Chairman and the non-executive directors were able to 'hold the ring' on behalf of the shareholder – the Government.

Thus there was no suggestion of animosity, but the Board as a whole had necessarily to look at the buy-out proposal from a different viewpoint than the proposers. When the executives first put the proposition to the Board it was treated as an idea that needed a good deal more flesh put on the bones before it could be adopted as a serious course of action. Even later, when flesh had been added to the original bones, the Board still cautioned the executives to keep at least one eye on the Government's goal: an Offer for Sale. There was indeed a Board view that a sale to the staff would effectively be a sale to a single purchaser, which would be difficult to justify when the directors had been politicking with the Government, to considerable effect, against a single-purchaser solution.

Fears were also expressed that new initiatives from NFC

(deputy chairman and chief executive), Mr B. R. Hayward† (National Carriers Group managing director), Mr F. S. Law, Mr J. D. Mather† (Special Traffics Group managing director), Mr P. G. Scott, Mr J. E. B. Sieve, Mr P. H. Spriddell, Sir Ronald Swayne, Mr J. K. Watson† (Finance director) and Mr D. H. White† (BRS Group managing director). (Those marked † were full-time NFC executives.)

might prompt new ideas on the part of the Government. But even by the end of 1979 the top executives were taking the view that a group which had increased its turnover from £291 million in 1975 to £417 million in 1979 – during which period the number of staff had been clipped from nearly 45,000 to just under 35,000 – must be moving in the right direction, and must intrinsically be worth more than the £50 million to £60 million that Schroders was estimating as its likely stock market value by that stage.

It was to be two years from these early misgivings to the point at which the Government finally agreed the purchase concept – on October 17 1981 – and even then there were substantial, and possibly insurmountable, problems ahead. The deal was conditional on the Consortium being able to raise sufficient money from the employees to finance the bulk of the ordinary share capital (equity), and it would also require a new Companies Act to make possible the preferred scheme – one which would make NFC's own shareholders clear masters of the situation. By one of those quirks of nature, which happen in real life, just such legislation was in preparation in a completely different Government Department: the 1981 Companies Act which was passed just in time.

But that is the benefit of hindsight: to look at a minefield from behind – once it has been negotiated. Far more frightening is approaching it from the other side; this was the prospect facing NFC's executives, and subsequently its directors, almost a year before the Corporation became a company – let alone being bought by a consortium.

No-one can put a firm date on the conception of the buy-out idea. Philip Mayo, director of legal services at NFC, remembers thinking or saying (he is not quite sure which) towards the end of 1979: 'Hell, at this price we could buy it ourselves.' Peter Thompson regards a golfing weekend in Wales in the spring of 1980 as the crucial time when vague ideas were brought into the open and the harsh question asked: 'Could we really do it?'

James Watson, NFC's finance director, calls this 'the folklore answer', meaning only that it is the version of events that is most likely to go down in posterity as to when the idea was born. Certainly it was an important occasion in view of what came later. Twelve senior executives of the group congregated at Eric Shortland's cottage in Wales (Mr Shortland was at that time managing director of Morton's (BRS) Ltd, a small company in the BRS Group). The others present were either on the executive committee or were managing directors of major NFC subsidiaries.

Peter Thompson explains that the weekends at Eric Shortland's cottage at Aberdovey, near a first-class golf course, date back to 1973 when the then senior managers of BRS who played golf used to have self-catering breaks there twice a year. One of the rules of the weekend was that it was purely relaxation for 12 of the managers who happened to like each other's company, and normally no serious business was discussed. He recalls:

> However, at one of these weekends shortly after Schroders had advised the Government that the price it could expect for the NFC was £50 million–£60 million, a heated discussion took place over the dinner prepared by Brian Hayward, National Carriers group managing director. The heart of the argument was that, with all the improvements that the group of managers knew had been achieved but which hadn't yet manifested themselves in improved profit, the business was surely worth more than £50 million–£60 million – and why not buy it for themselves?

There is no doubt that at this particular gathering the whole idea of a buy-out solution was given an airing but, as Peter Thompson stresses, at this point it was only a discussion. What was discussed at that stage was the idea of a management buy-out rather than a staff buy-out: there was still a very long way to go. Certainly no action followed from that conversation piece – and the two men who would eventually have to tackle the legal and financial problems, Philip Mayo and James

Watson, were not even present on that occasion. After that weekend the topic went into limbo for something like six months. Undoubtedly, however, the seeds of the idea had been sown.

These seeds were to shoot in the autumn of 1980. In spite of the financial uncertainties facing NFC (1980 profit before tax was to turn out at just £400,000 against £10 million the previous year) Schroders had not further downgraded the price it expected the Corporation to fetch on the stock market. What the bank had done, however, was to reassess its views on timing: although these views were not officially confirmed to the Board of NFC until January 26 1981, it was clear much earlier that Schroders was now looking at mid-1982 as the earliest possible date for an Offer for Sale, and would certainly prefer the option of 1983.

As was to happen again later, a number of things occurred in a relatively short space of time around this period. National Freight Company Ltd had been incorporated on June 30 under the 1980 Transport Act with a nominal capital of £1,000. On September 8 this was increased to £5 million, and the balance of the unissued shares was issued to the Secretary of State for Transport on October 1 at the same time as Statutory Order No. 1380 (1980) (The National Freight Corporation (Transfer of Undertaking) Order) came into effect. That piece of statutory jargon meant that the Corporation ceased to exist and the Company took over all its rights, properties and obligations. With the creation of the new equity in NFC Ltd, the Corporation's £100 million debt to the Government was extinguished.

As soon as the company was formed Sir Robert Lawrence and Mr Victor Paige were appointed directors, and on September 17 a full working Board with a further ten directors was appointed – including five full-time executive directors led by Peter Thompson as deputy chairman and chief executive: controls on directors' salaries, and constraints on areas of operation, disappeared at the same time as nationalised industry (i.e. Corporation) status. Within days of the company taking over, it received the body-blow that played a major part in Schroders' reconsideration of the timing of a possible flotation. The Department of Transport sanctioned the idea of Sir Peter Parker, chairman of British Rail, to axe the British Rail Express Parcels Service. Providing the road-based part of this service had been NFC's biggest single contract, and the loss of it would cost NFC £25 million in profitable turnover, and the same amount in cash for restructuring costs.

It was against this background that some months later Peter Thompson formally raised the possibility of a management buy-out – at a meeting of the NFC chairman's committee on February 18 1981. Present at that meeting were Sir Robert Lawrence, Victor Paige, James Watson, Philip Mayo, and of course Peter Thompson himself. This, according to Mr Thompson, 'was the first time we felt we could take the idea seriously.' The matter was duly raised before the full Board in March 1981 – and met with a cautious reception.

This was the point at which the full Board said, effectively, 'go and do some more work on the idea'. It was also the time that mild conflicts of interest began to develop, in the sense that the Board as a whole was exercising stewardship of the company on behalf of the controlling shareholder – the Secretary of State for Transport – but within that Board was a group of executives who wanted to explore alternative solutions to the Offer for Sale route expressly outlined by the Government. As already stated, there was no question of disagreement – as was subsequently proved beyond doubt in the way that non-executive and part-time executive directors played an important role in bringing the consortium idea to fruition. But prior to the crystallisation of the concept there was a certain uneasiness about which role each individual should play.

Eventually the Consortium was to end up with an official Organising Committee of 14 people while others, not committed to the Consortium in any official capacity, were to see that the Government, the Company and its pensioners were all treated fairly. Still others were to put in a great deal of work on property, legal, and financial considerations. But at the start the Consortium idea lay unofficially in half a dozen or so hands, and they were busy with a series of discussions in The Merton Centre headquarters in Bedford to put the necessary flesh on the bones of the original concept.

Peter Thompson describes these early meetings as 'unstructured'. He, James Watson and Philip Mayo and three or four Group managing directors of major subsidiaries hashed the idea over time and time again until gradually some sort of structure emerged.

This 'Cabal' of ideas men, as it was later dubbed, settled a number of key issues during this period, but none was more important than what Peter Thompson calls 'the change from a management buy-out to the charisma of the concept of a staff buy-out.' He recalls vividly how, at one of these freewheeling meetings, Ted Wall, managing director of the international division of the company, produced a rough guesstimate of just how much a notional consortium could hope to raise from each level of management and staff. Gradually too, it became clear that to James Watson would fall the task of working out just what sort of financial structure would be workable, and to Philip Mayo the job of trying to translate ideas into legal structure and check their feasibility in terms of the various relevant provisions of the Companies Acts and any other impinging legislation.

The charisma of a staff buy-out as opposed to a management buy-out developed in the minds of the Cabal to almost 'vision' proportions. Apart from the obvious political and commercial attractions – less chance of political reprisals in the event of a change in government, and less danger of a successful predatory bid from a disinterested outsider – it seemed to offer the prospect of an entirely new type of industrial structure.

It would be conventional in that the Board would still be responsible to shareholders, yet unconventional in the sense

The Organising Committee. Rear row, left to right:
Edward Wall, *Managing Director, National Freight Company (International) Ltd*
Geoffrey Pygall, *Group Managing Director, Pickfords Group*
Brian Cottee, *Head of Communication Services, National Freight Company Ltd*
Peter Thompson, *Deputy Chairman and Chief Executive, National Freight Company Ltd and leader of the Organising Committee*
David White, *Group Managing Director, British Road Services Group*
Michael Sweet, *Director of Corporate Planning, National Freight Company Ltd*
Kenneth Cook, *Director of Administration, National Freight Company Ltd*

Centre row, left to right:
John Copland, *Managing Director, Scottish Freight Company Ltd*
Bryan Wilson, *Director of Personnel, National Freight Company Ltd*
John Mather, *Group Managing Director, Special Traffics Group*

Front row, left to right:
Philip Mayo, *Director of Legal Services, National Freight Company Ltd*
* Arthur Smith, *Group Managing Director, Roadline Group*
James Watson, *Director of Finance, National Freight Company Ltd*
Brian Hayward, *Group Managing Director, National Carriers Group*

* Arthur Smith *left the employment of the NFC Group on November 30 1981*

that, although the shareholders were members of the group's own workforce, it would be a properly constituted company and not a co-operative with decisions taken on a concensus basis. (As Peter Thompson points out the co-operative solution probably could not have worked anyway in a group with over 700 operating units scattered the length and breadth of the country.) Perhaps the most important of all, the concept could begin to break down the 'us and them' philosophy between workforce and management which has constantly bedevilled British industry.

There was of course a danger of another 'us and them' between shareholders and non-shareholders, and meanwhile a host of other problems loomed on the horizon. First the Board would have to be convinced – then banks, the Government, trade unions. Most important of all – if the idea was to stand any chance of success – a substantial proportion of the workforce and the pensioners of NFC would have to be convinced. Communication from here on in was going to be a crucial factor in almost every quarter.

The decision to go ahead from this point was a decision to put a first foot in the minefield. Those involved knew where they wanted to go, but they did not know the route – or even if there was a route. There was an unspoken fear that if they had tried to tackle all the problems at once the project might seem too big altogether. Sensibly, it was decided to take each difficulty as it arose.

James Watson and Philip Mayo had to work closely together: financial solutions would be of little use if they did not stand up legally and, by the same token, legal solutions were no good if they did not stand up financially.

They worked fast. On February 27 1981 a document, 'Principles of a management-led consortium' was produced and circulated by Philip Mayo. It was marked: 'Strictly confidential, not to be copied.' It outlined three solutions – the third of which was to be remarkably close to the final outcome. Initially only five people had sight of it: Messrs Thompson,

Mather, Watson, Mayo and Wall: the five whose thoughts and conversations were behind these first proposals.

James Watson recalls his first reactions when Peter Thompson originally raised the idea of the buy-out with him:

> The initial thing I had to consider was whether we could raise a sum in the region of £50 million, and secondly could we do that and still retain control of the business? Thirdly I had to decide whether we could produce a corporate structure that would make sense financially and, fourthly, – perhaps most importantly – could we provide a reasonable return to investors?

It was this last point which concerned James Watson most: he formed the view that with the financial backing of 'a friendly institution' the mechanics of the deal were not impossible in financial terms, but there was a moral decision to be taken as well. Could the emerging Consortium honestly recommend its employees to invest their savings in their own jobs?

It was a difficult time (one of many) that tested more than one person's conscience. In many ways it was a 'Catch 22' problem: formal consultation with government, legal and financial advisers could hardly take place without firm proposals on the table but, equally, it was not an easy job to prepare proposals without such consultation – and without premature disclosure to possible competitors. Added to this was the rogue factor of just which forecasts NFC could realistically offer, given uncertainties over trading conditions and – in what was almost bound to be a highly geared organisation if it came into being – the movement in interest rates.

In the meantime other strands were being woven into the overall tapestry. Still with a public Offer for Sale in mind the full Board in the autumn of 1980 had looked for an advertising and financial public relations firm. While several of the main subsidiaries such as Pickfords and BRS were individually well known, they were not publicly identified with NFC, and the

Corporation's deliberately chosen role as a largely anonymous holding company made it an unknown quantity in the investment world, as indeed elsewhere. Clearly if NFC was to be opened to private investment, the market needed to be made familiar with the nature of the business and its constituent parts. 'As part of the preparation for financial PR activity next year' (the quote is part of an internal memorandum from Brian Cottee to the Chairman) three large agencies were invited to make presentations to NFC. As a result McCann Erickson, one of the world's biggest advertising agencies, and its financial PR company, Universal McCann, was chosen – and retained initially as financial public relations adviser. Little did it know at that stage that the job it would eventually be expected to do was a far cry from the task it had originally pitched for. Now, in early 1981, it was about to find out.

In January 1981, Schroders confirmed, officially, its rescheduling further into the future of the proposed timing of a possible stock market flotation. Following that, on February 18, the Board of NFC met to consider seriously the alternatives to the Government's preferred solution. The next few days saw intensive effort to produce other options. The original options, although evaluated by February 23, were not circulated until February 27, and then on the restricted basis.

These precautions are understandable, because at that stage 'Principles of a management-led consortium' was akin to political dynamite. Referring to the Government's commitment on privatisation as it related to NFC, the four-page document stated: 'This is a *political* commitment and is not related to financial considerations, but the price obtained must not appear to be totally derisory.' That, one of nine of 'the most important factors giving rise to the proposal' (of a management-led buy-out), struck at the heart of the matter: because now that the Government was committed to fund historical pension deficiencies (by then estimated at £45 million) it would not receive much change after expenses even if the Consortium managed to raise a gross £55 million.

The other 'important factors' – such as the state of the economy and stock market and the danger of the Government seeking alternative solutions for political reasons if flotation were to be delayed too long – have already been mentioned. Taking all these factors into consideration, the document concluded that the Secretary of State

may well respond favourably to a proposal which:

i.   Offers the prospect of an earlier disposal with less exposure to outside factors.
ii. Provides the same net proceeds to the Government.
iii. Achieves a reasonably wide spread of ownership, and
iv. Demonstrates management commitment.

A management consortium could do all of these things. Providing that the net proceeds were reasonably close to those likely to be obtained by a flotation, the involvement of the employees would probably be enough to remove the necessity for any sort of tendering procedure.

The last point – concerning tendering – was indeed a tender issue for NFC, and was likely to prove an equal problem to the Government. From the company's point of view, the idea of an offer by tender had been examined as another alternative solution to ward off a possible break-up in the likely event of an Offer for Sale being impossible within the required time scale, but had been regarded unfavourably since there would be no way in which the company could influence who would be its eventual owner. The Government too was against a tender offer but the embarrassment of agreeing to sell to a consortium without giving others the opportunity to make an offer could lead to accusations of selling off national assets on the cheap: particularly since the net proceeds after funding pension deficiencies would appear tiny compared with the book value of NFC's assets. NFC's embryo consortium hoped that a sale to employees would help draw the political sting from that issue as far as the Government was concerned (although it later took the belt and braces precaution of having the asset values and stock market valuation of some prominent public companies compared – and found the results satisfactory: the discrepancy in the market's valuation of these other groups was reassuringly inconsistent).

Considering that 'Principles of a Management-led consortium' was drawn up in February 1981, the principles it laid down for the proposed consortium bear an uncanny resemblance to the eventual outcome in overall terms, if not in precise detail.

Five were listed:

i.   Control should be vested, initially in the management, ultimately in the employees.

ii. Subject to the above, equity participation by e.g. institutions . . . would be permitted.

iii. The structure should enable a Stock Exchange quotation to be obtained later.

iv. All existing senior and management staff would be expected to participate and participation would be a condition of employment for future management and senior staff entrants [a condition subsequently dropped]. Other employees would be given an opportunity to invest.

v.   Employee shares would initially be transferable only between employees at a valuation. It would probably be necessary to set up a trust to act as a pool/buyer of last resort to provide shares for new entrants or buy shares of e.g. deceased or leaving employees.

Inevitably at this early stage, the organisational and financial structures proposed were vague and all that was put forward was a possible structure which did not, in the end, materialise. The principle of control by the consortium was, however, embodied – although at that time a figure of between 51 per cent and 75 per cent of the equity in the consortium's hands was mooted.

But even the crude (in relative terms) financial calculations turned out to be not too far from the mark. Starting from the Schroders' £50 million–£60 million estimate of gross proceeds from a market flotation, the paper took the middle figure of £55 million as a starting point, knocked off £2.5 million for expenses involved in a flotation and a further £45 million for pension deficiencies, leaving net proceeds for Government of £7.5 million.

The assumption had already been made that the Government was prepared to accept a net £7.5 million to sell off NFC, and that its main priority would be the time-scale of the operation. In simple terms, the first bidder to come up with that amount would have a good chance of success. But it was recognised that, in the same way that the sell-off was politically motivated, the way it was presented would also have to be politically acceptable. The following quote indicates the delicacy of the problem and the resulting complications that could have arisen had NFC pursued the suggested course. It was a carefully phrased document:

> . . . it might be thought that it would be possible to accept the (pension) deficiency in the company and simply pay the Government what it would expect to get, net, out of a flotation, say £7.5 million. This ignores the political difficulties of the Government appearing to hand over assets worth over £100 million for less than a tenth of that. It is therefore suggested that the company should offer loan stock to the extent necessary to eliminate the pension deficiency, with the remainder being equity, of which the majority would be held by the management/employees. The Government would then pay the proceeds of the loan stock over to the pension funds, leaving the company to service and redeem it in due course.

On that basis the capital structure suggested was:

	£m
Equity held by employees	5
Equity held by institutions	2.5
Loan stock	45
	52.5

Given subsequent alterations in profit forecasts, the pension deficiency, and the unforeseen pitfalls that were to crop up, that original rough assessment was to prove remarkably close to the final outcome. The very high level of gearing involved was explicitly admitted but, in spite of the recessionary state of the economy, this did not discourage the five men responsible for the document: on NFC's forecast recovery the gearing could only work in their favour.

From the preparation of that original document the main activity lay in continually refining it. By March 10 the paper was ready to go to the Chairman's Committee, and there were few, but significant, changes. In the first place the original general thinking had been honed down to two clear options: Option A involved the raising of between £50 million and £52.5 million with between £5 million and £7.5 million being equity, and the rest loan stock which would be used to pay off the pension deficiency. Option B was to raise between £5 million and £7.5 million being equity to pay the Government and for the company to accept the pensions deficiency.

The possible scaling down of the equity (the value of the total capital structure held by shareholders who own the company, as opposed to loan stock holders who simply lend the company money) from a firm £7.5 million reflected a growing conviction that the actual open market price would be towards the lower end of Schroders' original £50 million to £60 million bracket. Also, a further snag had cropped up in relation to Option B: as well as the likelihood of it being unacceptable to the Government, it would probably not be acceptable in another area:

The Trustees of the Pension Funds would be unlikely to

agree to forego a lump sum in favour of a provision in the books of a non-Government-backed company (unless the provision could be secured in some way).

Effectively, therefore, Option B was dropped, and attention concentrated on the possibilities of Option A.

The only other major change was to spell out the advantages and disadvantages of a management-led consortium. Briefly, the advantages were that it offered the chance of an earlier and more certain route to privatisation than the alternatives, which would suit both management and the Government; a staff-controlled company would offer better protection against a predatory bid from outsiders than a widespread public share-holding; there would be greater staff and management commitment to make a success of 'their own' company; and – last but by no means least – it would make renationalisation by a future Labour government much more difficult.

This last point was certainly a major consideration as far as NFC was concerned (and remains so to this day). It is a reasonable assumption, also, that it subsequently became an added attraction of the buy-out solution as far as the Government was concerned. Indeed, much later – in the spring of 1982 – a draft statement 'A Transport Policy for Labour' admitted that the buy-out solution to privatise NFC might prove a thorn in the Party's side in achieving its stated belief 'that a publicly-owned share of the road haulage industry is essential for the health of the industry . . .'.

That document went on: '. . . It might not be appropriate to establish a new organisation to rival NFC and yet it may be assumed there could be resistance amongst NFC employees to the renationalisation of *their* company.' (My italics.)

As recorded earlier, the management-led consortium proposal went to the full Board on Wednesday, March 18 1981, by which time a detailed financial evaluation of Option A had been appended, drawn up by James Watson. There were still various alternative approaches available under Option A, but basically the figures were that NFC management and staff should raise £5 million in equity to pay the Government, and raise £45 million in loans to fund the pension deficiency (through the Government). This would leave a group with shareholders' funds of £126.3 million and borrowings of £100.3 million – giving a gearing ratio of just under 80 per cent. The gearing ratio represents the proportion of fixed interest debt to equity. The importance of it is that interest has to be paid on fixed interest debt however well or badly the company performs, and it takes precedence over other payments to investors. Payment on equity capital (ordinary shares) varies with the performance of the company and is paid out of residual (shareholders') funds. The higher the gearing the more money is left for shareholders in good years, but the less there is for them in bad years. On the group's forecasts, pre-tax profit for the year ended January 1 1982 would be £14 million, and after dividends and Advance Corporation Tax there would be a retained profit of £12.6 million. Various alternative means of raising the £45 million loan were also sketched out.

The full proposal and evaluation was 'considered' by the Board and referred back to the executive committee. It was not to be until April 14 that the Board finally agreed that the best route to follow was the purchase of National Freight Company Ltd from the Government by a management-led consortium.

By this time the 'consortium' had effectively become the Organising Committee (pictured on page 36) which was to see the concept through to reality.

4

THE BARGAINING
BEGINS

I had no illusions about what a tough assignment the
consortium was facing. My view was: 'You've taken on a hell
of a task, and I will help you all I can.'

> Quote from a 1982 interview with Sir Robert
> ('Bobbie') Lawrence, who was Chairman of
> NFC Ltd when the Board gave its blessing
> to the consortium solution.

Even before the Board of NFC had given the green light to the
consortium idea some discreet feelers had been put out to test
possible reactions. On a strictly confidential and unofficial
basis a small number of top managers (essentially, those who
became the organising committee) were sounded out in general
terms about the possibility of management and staff participation. Obviously, on the principle that a secret shared is a secret
lost this process had its dangers, and a leak at that stage could
have killed the whole thing stone dead. On the other hand, to
achieve the £5 million equity input envisaged at that stage
would require the equivalent of an average investment of £200
by *every one* of the NFC's 25,000 employees, and if the top
managers were unlikely to be enthusiastic about the concept
of participation, then the idea was a non-starter anyway.

Fortunately for the aspiring consortium leaders the reaction was universally favourable, and there was no breach in security. (On a rule of thumb basis the risk of a leak increases in geometric proportion to the number of people who are in on a secret. It is quite remarkable how well the consortium idea was kept under wraps until the first official announcement in June 1981 – by which time the number of people 'in the know' ran very comfortably into three figures.)

While these cautious internal temperatures were being taken external pulses were also being felt. On March 30 1981 the concept was put to Mr Hugh Ashton, the senior Schroder Wagg director involved with NFC and, at least according to NFC sources, he seemed 'taken aback' at the suggestion. Nevertheless, at a second meeting on April 8, Schroders conceded that some sort of scheme could be on the cards involving institutional backing and employee participation. The Schroders' concept was based on a minority employee participation which was not at all what Peter Thompson and his colleagues had in mind, but at that stage the concession that some sort of buy-out could be feasible was sufficient.

It fell to Bobbie Lawrence to surmount the next hurdle although he was not, and never was to be, a member of the Cabal. The day after the second meeting with Schroders, on April 9, Sir Robert had a meeting with the Secretary of State for Transport, Norman Fowler, and informed him that work was being undertaken within NFC on the possibility of a management-led buy-out as an alternative to the Offer for Sale. Mr Fowler agreed at that meeting that further studies should be undertaken as to the feasibility of that solution, and underlined the message that had already been relayed by members of his Department: he wanted privatisation of NFC to be accomplished before July 1982.

Undoubtedly these three 'pro-consortium' indicators played a part in the Board's decision to press the 'go' button to concentrate on a consortium-based solution. Much later, in his chairman's statement accompanying the 1981 accounts of NFC, Sir Robert said:

> Like the change from Corporation to Company, the management-led employee buy-out was supported by the Board as the best course for the business, its employees and its customers in the prevailing circumstances. The action taken by the Secretary of State, both in the transfer to a limited company and in paving the way for employee ownership, was appreciated by the Board.

But at the outset, in April 1981, Sir Robert was absolutely correct in his surmise that the embryo consortium had taken on 'one hell of a task'. There had never been a management buy-out of this magnitude, and the full concept of a buy-out with some 25,000 staff plus families and pensioners eligible to participate in the purchase of a company with a turnover well in excess of £400 million was little short of revolutionary. The Consortium, headed by Peter Thompson and aided by his two principal lieutenants, finance director James Watson and legal director Philip Mayo, had to convince somebody to lend them around £50 million on a medium term basis, underwrite the internal offer for sale, and provide another £30 million or so in overdraft facilities to give NFC adequate working capital. The weapons in their armoury were a Board which included a number of experienced, respected, and well-connected non-executive directors; a management team in which they had great faith, but outsiders would need convincing; and projections on organisational structure and financial projects which would have to stand up to the toughest possible scrutiny before anyone would part with the sort of money they were seeking.

Even in February, confidential documents referred to the possibility of looking to other banks than Schroders, and on April 15 Frank Law, one of NFC's non-executive directors, wrote to the chairman saying, *inter alia*:

The second problem will undoubtedly be the finding of the necessary finance, and if I may advise here, we should not be satisfied with just Schroders, but should also talk to one or two other banks, to see what they can come up with.

Independently, James Watson in his role as finance director had come to a similar conclusion:

Having talked to Schroders I gradually formed the view that what we needed was not a merchant bank, but a clearing bank with a strong merchant banking arm.

Frank Law (left) and Victor Paige were among the experienced, respected and well-connected directors who contributed to the early discussions, particularly in the political and banking areas, and later were prominent in holding the ring on behalf of the Government.

James Watson already had contacts with Barclays Bank, but
it was Sir Robert Lawrence who opened the batting. Replying
to Frank Law's letter, Bobbie Lawrence said:

> Your point about talking to other banks besides Schroders is
> well taken and I have arranged for a meeting with Lord
> Camoys of Barclays Merchant Bank on 24th April as an
> opening gambit.

The whole story of the NFC buy-out is littered with 'crucial'
meetings, but none were more important than the first two with
BMB: in London on April 24, and in Bedford on April 29.

On Friday April 24 Sir Robert, Victor Paige, Peter Thompson and James Watson met with Lord Camoys, Ron Watson
(deputy managing director of BMB – and no relation to
James), Oliver Stocken (head of corporate advice at BMB) and
Michael Peterson (corporate advice director of the merchant
bank). The venue was BMB's headquarters in Gracechurch
Street in the City of London. The NFC directors outlined their
proposals, and a somewhat-stunned Barclays team retired to
consider their verdict: most things financial are possible within
the famous 'Square Mile' of the City – in its 1,000 years as a
leading world financial centre the City, collectively at least, can
reckon to have seen just about everything. It had not, however,
seen anything like this before.

Tom Camoys, in spite of his title, is not an ageing, benevolent
peer. You don't get to be managing director of an emerging,
relatively new merchant bank that way, and the date of that
first meeting was just eight days after his 41st birthday. He is a
shrewd and urbane man who needs no title to hold down his
job.

Neither Ron Watson nor Michael Peterson fit into the
erroneous identikit picture that most people have of smooth,
imperturbable merchant bankers lending millions of pounds
over a glass of port in the club. But Mr Watson has the self
assurance that is required of anyone who has to make swift –

and sometimes risky – decisions involving large sums of money.

Michael Peterson, who arrived at BMB via Warburgs, one of the members of the elite Accepting Houses Committee, can best be described as a firecracker: he radiates the impression of enormous enthusiasm and fires off ideas, decisions and opinions rather like a machine gun.

I sketch in these subjective observations because it was these men who, after a brief recess, decided that it was worth having a further look at the highly unusual proposition being offered to them. NFC could have knocked at many other doors and been turned down flat. Even so, BMB wanted a great deal of convincing, and the NFC was given just five days to produce a presentation in Bedford to prove to the bank that the proposition was feasible.

The following Wednesday, April 29, a five-man team from Barclays Merchant Bank boarded an early-morning train from St Pancras station to Bedford. In addition to Mr Watson and Mr Peterson there was Graham Williams who, as a director of Barclays Development Capital, would end up holding shares on behalf of Barclays (technically at least) if the deal went ahead; Alan Brown, a clearing banker by background who would have to bear the brunt of negotiations with his own parent company; and Michael Hamer, an assistant director of BMB whose job it was to cast a detailed and critical eye on the group structure proposed by NFC.

By all accounts it was not a particularly optimistic quintet at that stage. Good bankers all, they felt that they were simply going through the motions of a deal that in all probability they would be forced to reject at the end of the day. By the end of that particular day – a memorable one for both NFC and BMB – the situation had changed dramatically: bankers do not commit themselves to large sums of money because they have been given a smooth, professional presentation, but the five went home sufficiently interested to pursue the concept in much greater detail.

Although no-one has specifically said so, it is fair to assume that the bankers were prepared for a 'nationalised industry' type presentation which would not meet normal commercial banking requirements. What they got was something quite different. But the NFC team was also wrong-footed: hours of preparation of contingency answers to detailed financial questions were to prove wasted at that stage: the bankers were interested in other things.

The working day kicked off with the required presentation by the NFC team, supported by a mass of information on slides. Victor Paige was in the chair, but the talking fell to the other four members: Messrs Thompson, Mayo, Sweet, and James Watson. Peter Thompson sketched out, in some detail, the buy-out concept and the Consortium corporate plan; Mr Sweet went into the details of how this would work at operational level. Not surprisingly, Philip Mayo concentrated on the legal aspect of the proposed deal and the work that had been undertaken in that department, while James Watson outlined NFC's ideas on the proposed financial structure, and internal budget forecasts for the immediate future.

There followed a lunch at which the group managing directors each spoke about their areas of the business, and in the afternoon it was to be Barclays' turn to ask questions. Having been convinced of the commercial acumen of the NFC team in the morning session they did not – again at this stage – want to know more figures: they wanted to know more about the people involved, the depth of management – and the two 'p's', property and pensions.

Thompson, Mayo and Watson have all, independently, expressed surprise about the course that the afternoon session took: each was prepared for rigorous questioning on their facts, figures and ambitions, but not one of the three was prepared for the Barclays line of questioning.

From my own experience, I know that you can fudge figures even just by being over-optimistic in assumptions. What you cannot do is to fudge people, and it was an assessment of the people involved that was crucial to the Barclays decision. As Peter Thompson remarked later: 'They didn't so much want to know more about the figures, they wanted to know more about us and our management style'.

Notes taken at that afternoon meeting and a subsequent interview with Ron Watson confirm that assessment. In fact, Peter Thompson's forceful morning presentation was almost too much of a good thing as far as the bankers were concerned. Mr Watson recalls thinking: 'Is Peter Thompson too strong; is this a one-man-band?' Fortunately, the other presentations had done enough to convince the Barclays team that the top management was sound. Still, though, the bankers wanted confirmation and more detail.

Even in the morning session Barclays had asked some searching questions. They wanted to know how many senior managers there were in the group; how many people were eligible for bonuses related to achievement; what was the prospect on future redundancies; and how property within the group was valued.

In the afternoon they had something of a field day. The first thing they requested (effectively required) was the ages and backgrounds of the executive directors and, following that, the Barclays team wanted to know about management succession. To that end they requested dinner with some of NFC's 'high flyers', and also discussions with group managing directors coupled with visits to some of the operating companies. The underlying thinking is quite understandable: what would happen to the proposed Consortium if Peter Thompson fell under a bus – or for that matter one of his own lorries?

On the question of management Barclays went as far as to probe NFC's policy on graduate intake, but other, more fundamental issues were also raised. The following quotes are taken verbatim from NFC's own files:

General Points
A. It was necessary to analyse what form of banking

proposition Barclays Merchant Bank would make, and *the whole form of the banking proposition would hinge on the funding of the pension scheme*.

B. *Equity*

Mr. Thompson was in favour of NFC having 100 per cent equity; however, the point was made that a small shareholding by an institution such as Barclays might give greater confidence to smaller investors. Mr. Thompson stressed that the situation was not viable if Barclays wanted a majority shareholding. This was understood. Barclays might have to syndicate equity.

C. *Security*

Barclays enquired whether there were any strong objections on security. Mr. (James) Watson said he would rather not give security.

At this stage confidentiality was all. Although Schroders knew that NFC management was talking to another institution, the bank did not know who it was. Also Peter Thompson – ever eager to press on – wanted the Barclays decision by the middle of May, but Barclays, although eager to help, refused to commit itself to a specific timetable.

In fact the whole of May was to be taken up with detailed financial studies between James Watson and the bank's nominated representatives, plus bank meetings with the group managing directors and visits to their companies, including some of their operating branches. Also, Barclays, anxious to avoid any possible conflict of interest and not wishing to extend their financial commitment into yet another area, declined to take the lead in offering a special loan scheme for employees. (From an early stage the Cabal had realised that they would have to help employees to raise loans in order to invest – indeed, there was a view that even such aid would not induce people accustomed to putting their spare cash into building societies or savings banks to break this habit and participate in share purchase.)

Later, several banks, notably National Westminster, made available loan schemes to employees wishing to invest. Barclays, however, eventually became involved in a different way, using a trust scheme under Companies Acts provisions to make available, at arms length, the money to cover the employee loan scheme arranged by the Consortium, which allowed employees to borrow up to £200 interest-free in order to subscribe for up to 200 shares. Repayments were made through deductions from their pay over 12 months.

June 1981 saw a complete change in tempo, with everyone moving into top gear. June 5 saw one of the most important pieces of paper in the whole exercise: Barclays' conditional agreement to provide the necessary funds to finance the buy-out, and shortly after that on June 9 and 10 the triumvirate of Thompson, Watson and Mayo gave a highly confidential presentation in a Bedford hotel to around 120 of the most senior managers – regarded as essential in gauging support before putting a fuller proposal to Norman Fowler. (It was to be the first of some 700 presentations that were to be made to employees at all levels to outline and sell the idea.)

The enthusiastic response of the senior managers at this Bedford meeting enabled Peter Thompson to tell Norman Fowler that a bid could be put together, and June 18 was subsequently chosen as the date for a series of carefully timed revelations of the proposal to different audiences. On that day the NFC's 25,000 employees were handed a printed notice explaining the proposition; the relevant trade union leaders were told what was intended; and there was a joint NFC/BMB press conference in the City to announce the buy-out concept to a largely unsuspecting group of financial and trade journalists. Meanwhile the Secretary of State was telling the House of Commons and adding: 'This is an imaginative and exciting proposal and I have told the managers concerned that I hope it will prove possible to achieve such a sale'.

For much of the latter part of June, consultations were taking place with the three main unions involved with NFC: The Transport and General Workers' Union, the National Union of Railwaymen, and the Transport Salaried Staffs Association.

On June 24 the first meeting was held to start the mammoth task of preparing one of the most unusual prospectuses ever to be issued in the United Kingdom. That meeting involved NFC, bankers, solicitors and accountants and was to be the first of many that were to run right into January 1982.

This period was the start of a headlong rush that was to continue right into 1982. For every problem solved, at least two more seemed to crop up and it would be both impossible and incomprehensible to go into all the intricate detail: Barclays' original acceptance letter alone runs to a close-typed nine pages including appendices, and was based on a scheme which it was hoped would avoid falling foul of the dreaded Section 54 of the 1948 Companies Act.

In simple terms (which would give any good company lawyer heart failure) Section 54 stopped people buying a company with its own assets. It was designed to prevent fraud, but not designed to deal with NFC's situation in 1981. It was that Section 54 which prevented NFC giving Barclays security on bank loans backed by its properties. Companies Acts will crop up again in this book with almost monotonous regularity, but this brief synopsis is raised now because in June 1981 nobody seemed to realise the extent of the problems that the 1948 Act would cause until it was – almost miraculously – replaced by a 1981 Companies Act that solved the major difficulties.

But back to that all-important letter of June 5 from Mr Ron Watson of Barclays to Mr Peter Thompson of NFC:

> Further to our recent discussions I am pleased to confirm that in principle the Barclays Group wishes to give financial support to the proposed purchase of National Freight Company Ltd ('NFC') by its employees.

The terms outlined by Mr Watson involved four types of finance to 'NEWCO' as the Consortium was then termed. There was to be an underwriting facility of up to £4.375 million if employees did not subscribe for their full allotment of shares available – but the deal would be off if the management could not raise at least £2.5 million in cash from NFC members.

As part of the deal, Barclays Development Capital would expect to subscribe for between 10 per cent and 20 per cent of 'NEWCO's' capital, the parent company, Barclays Bank, would lend £40 million and the merchant bank £5 million to fund pension deficiencies, and an overdraft facility of up to £25 million would be made available.

Summing this up, Mr Watson said:

> From these elements we envisage that you will thus be able to assemble a bid of £52.5 million and finance your trading activities should your bid be accepted.

As the next chapter explains, this is a highly unusual banking proposition, particularly since, at that stage, Barclays was offering it off its own bat, with no syndication arranged involving other banks. That was to come later.

At the same time the bank was not giving 'owt for nowt' and there were some severe 'conditions precedent' on the arrangement. Apart from the £2.5 million minimum subscription, the bank also demanded that the top 13 managers should between them commit £250,000 (i.e. 10 per cent of the minimum), and that at least another 1,250 managers should come up with not less than £625,000. There were also stipulations about leasing agreements, the thorny problem of reorganising the parcels divisions following the loss of the BREPS contract and, wisely as it turned out, 'Counsel's approval of the overall scheme including the security and repayment arrangements for the various financial facilities.' (Section 54 again.) NFC was to pay for Barclay's valuation of property plus a general fee of £250,000 and Barclays would have to be satisfied about the composition of the NEWCO Board if NEWCO succeeded in taking over NFC Ltd.

Mr Watson's final paragraph in that letter is straightforward:

> I am delighted that we have been able to assemble this offer for you and hope you will agree that it provides a firm basis for you to commence official discussions with your employees and the Government.

The penultimate paragraph is less reassuring however:

> . . . As we have discussed previously, may we please be consulted regarding any press releases and any reference to the Barclays name in documents or papers provided to employees.

The bank had stuck its neck out, but not to the extent of wanting it chopped off.

That paragraph would hardly be worthy of mention – it is after all a reasonable request – if it had not been for an event on the morning of the day of the announcement Press conference.

Peter Thompson recalls that Barclays was not happy about standing on the same platform as NFC on June 18. Mr Watson's argument was that it was a little early to commit the bank; Mr Thompson pointed out that a Press conference which had only NFC members on the platform could turn out to be not much short of a fiasco. What price a buy-out solution if the funds were not committed?

Barclays gave way on that issue, and the resulting press coverage was favourable: financial journalists are usually receptive to new ideas that make sense – and are well presented. But behind the scenes for the next few months a certain amount of tension was to develop between NFC's consortium and its merchant bank. Mr Thompson had the problem of convincing a high proportion of something like 40,000 employees and pensioners that the buy-out idea was a good idea – and wanted to get that message across as quickly as possible. He wanted to tell NFC people everything.

Barclays, later supported by the other banks who were eventually to syndicate the loan agreements, wanted everything done not just within the letter of the law, but also within the spirit of the 'Yellow Peril' – the London Stock Exchange Requirements for the Listing of Securities for Quotation, even though the prospect of a stock market quote was at least five years in the future. In the cauldron atmosphere that developed towards the end of 1981, Peter Thompson and Ron Watson developed a healthy respect for each other in terms of hard bargaining.

In retrospect both can smile about it. Mr Watson pays Mr Thompson the compliment of being a communicator on a par with the almost legendary Ernie Harrison of Racal. For his part Peter Thompson says wryly:

> Since we were dealing with top banks we had to dance to their tune. All I was doing was occasionally seeking to play our own music.

But while management and bankers were gradually settling down together, all was not well in discussions with the trades unions. In addition to the three unions already mentioned, two others were consulted: the United Road Transport Union (URTU) and the Amalgamated Union of Engineering Workers (AUEW). Given the unions' links with the Labour Party, and that Party's implacable opposition to the Conservative Party's programme of 'privatisation' it is hardly surprising that NFC was not able to stir up much official union enthusiasm for the proposed buy-out. Indeed the fact that four out of the five unions consulted eventually gave at least grudging approval (and one gave active support) to the NFC solution to the problem could be regarded as a success – but the dissenting union was the biggest, the Transport and General Workers.

Nothing is ever simple about union negotiations in this country. The bargaining process is cumbersome as a rule, and also political and financial aims tend to get horribly mixed up. The fact that NFC had to deal regularly with five unions (and nine in all) is simply an indication of the unusual structure of the company – and of the British trade union system.

This book is about NFC's buy-out, not about politics and the trade union system, but to be brutally frank, those people who followed the doctrinaire advice of the TGWU to have nothing to do with the buy-out have missed out on an investment in their own company that increased in value to almost two and a half times its original price in the course of a year, together with net cash dividends amounting to 17 per cent of the original investment. There was, of course, no guarantee of that performance at the outset, but that was the situation which had emerged at the time of writing.

NFC decided on Union consultation early in June 1981 and, to quote Bryan Wilson, NFC's director of personnel,

This was done by a series of meetings in and outside the Machinery [his capital 'M'] commencing with a meeting of the Joint Trade Union Advisory Council on June 18, 1981.

By all accounts it was a disappointing meeting. That council is staffed only by top NFC executives and union representatives at general secretary and assistant general secretary level: since the NUR was in conference at Plymouth and the TGWU in conference in Brighton, the union side was represented only by the URTU, the AUEW and the TSSA. NFC knew that this would be the case, and dispatched Brian Hayward, group MD of National Carriers, to brief the NUR in Plymouth, while Jack Mather, group MD of the Special Traffics Group, went to talk to Alex Kitson, deputy general secretary of the TGWU, in Brighton.

To give some idea of the complexities involved I quote NFC's personnel director in full:

> The general reaction of that meeting (i.e. the London meeting involving the three unions who were able to be represented) was that although the union representatives did not like the idea of our company returning to the private sector it was recognised that this was the Government's intention and therefore if that was accepted as a given fact the particular method proposed by the company management appeared to be the most favourable option open.
>
> This meeting was followed by a formal meeting of the NFC Machinery of Negotiation in the afternoon, held at National Staff Council level. Similar meetings were held in the National Carriers' Machinery which has remained a separate entity since the National Freight Corporation came into being.
>
> Following these meetings requests were received from the NUR, the TSSA and TGWU for fuller explanation of our intentions. There was a special briefing of the full NUR Executive Committee on June 22 1981 in the Boardroom of the NUR Head Office when Mr Thompson and his senior team addressed the Executive Committee and answered questions. Representatives of the TGWU, including Alex Kitson, Jack Ashwell and the union's Research and Finance Officer came to the NFC's City Road, London, office for a similar briefing on June 30 1981, and the full TSSA Executive also came to the Merton Centre on July 1 1981 to receive a briefing likewise.

Even that was by no means the end of the story as far as union negotiations were concerned. The NUR decided to welcome the proposals as 'the only way to keep the NFC intact'. The TSSA was rather less fulsome: its Executive Committee 'noted the initiative of the NFC consortium regarding the introduction of private capital', but then went on to a three-way hedge-betting exercise.

'Nevertheless,' it continued, 'in view of the intransigent attitude of the present Government, believes it to be the best of the various alternatives'. That could be considered a favourable response, but: 'It also considers that any decision to invest is one to be made by the individual employee'. Neutral, but again, *but*: 'Attention must be drawn to TSSA policy that where the present Government de-nationalises transport undertakings, then these must be renationalised *without compensation* (my italics) by the next Labour Government'. Certainly not favourable to NFC's ambitions, and I would hate to be a TSSA member who had to make the decision on the basis of – yes this is the best idea going, but we will do our best to make sure you lose your investment when a Labour Government gets back into power.

The URTU not only accepted the buy-out as the best solution in the circumstances but offered space in its union newspaper for an explanation of the scheme and its objectives.

The TGWU had little problem with its attitude. After several days of discussion, during which the NFC was not at all certain which way the union would go, it came down firmly against. While Alex Kitson initially expressed the view that the union must oppose any form of privatisation, he recognised that if it *had* to happen, then the NFC Consortium solution was preferable to the likely alternatives. But the official view of that union – expressed in a letter dated June 30, and a press release (from Alex Kitson) dated July 9, emphasised the TGWU's opposition.

The views expressed by the TGWU are couched in terms which make a refreshing contrast to the bald facts and figures which were being discussed by management, bankers and the Government. For the sake of brevity only the press release from Mr Kitson is quoted here, but the release itself is quoted in full in the interests of accuracy:

The TGWU's Finance and General Purposes Committee Meeting today held detailed discussions about the proposed selling-off of the National Freight Corporation, and expressed its total opposition of this act of asset-stripping against the public sector of the road haulage industry.

The F & GP decided to fight the sell-off both in the interest of protecting its members jobs (*sic*) and protecting public enterprise against the ravages of a desperate Government aiming to bolster its sagging Treasury finances by short-sighted and politically-motivated asset-stripping.

The F & GP declared that it would support opposition to the sell-off by its membership and would fight the proposal through all available channels including through the TUC and the Labour Party in co-operation with its own Parliamentary Group.

The TGWU is also very concerned about the prospect that workers in the industry could be offered small shareholdings under one of the possible sell-off schemes.

In the TGWU's view share purchases for the workers are aimed at undermining opposition to the asset-stripping of the public sector, and would result in worker shareholders subsequently being involved in further selling-off of their own assets and jobs when private capital has a clearer picture of the choice assets which it wants to extract from the vast NFC operation.

'The shares likely to be on offer are going to be cheques that can only be cashed by redundancies and sales of equipment which the workforce depend on' stated Alex Kitson, Deputy General Secretary.

'In effect, the worker shareholders would have no real control. They would be a conscripted jury with no option but to pass their own death sentences when the NFC is further asset stripped.

'What could be on offer is a phoney element of control, adding up to a political con-trick staged by Transport Minister Norman Fowler, who is desperate to put trojan horses into the trade union camp. This aim is to confuse the stand which the trade union and labour movement must take against the destruction of public enterprise.

'Worker shares arising in this sort of situation, under this Government are a meal ticket to the dole queue. The TGWU believes that extreme caution should be exercised in assessing any such schemes, which are aimed to provide a desperately-needed diversion for a government which is becoming increasingly aware of the opposition to its whole asset-stripping strategy' stated Alex Kitson.

That press release, backed up by previous letters to NFC union officials and TGWU members could have done the buy-out a lot of damage, since the letters emphasised the union's active opposition to employees buying shares, together with its own policy of renationalisation under a Labour Government. In the event the damage was not too great outside of the South East of England: in spite of all the legal problems the financiers moved a little quicker than the union, and a TGWU delegates conference to discuss ways of dissuading employees from buying shares was actually convened – most embarrassingly – for the day after subscription lists were closed on the offer, which in the event was over-subscribed.

The TGWU remained intransigent to the end, but by the time the prospectus had been published other unions' attitudes had softened. The NUR maintained its firm opposition to denationalisation, while an extension of public ownership in transport remained a fundamental part of the Union's policy. But its welcome for the Consortium initiative had extended to seeking assurances that the interests of members who had purchased shares in NFC 'should be safeguarded in any future Labour Government legislation. Discussions are being arranged by the NUR with the Labour Party and the TUC to sort this out.'

The TSSA's uncompromising statement on its general policy of renationalisation without compensation at least appeared to be hedged in an interview in the TSSA Journal with General Secretary Mr Tom Jenkins. While stating: 'The TSSA Committee considers that any decision to invest in the NFC is one which can only be made by the individual employee', he made it quite clear that the aim of the TSSA would be to ensure that the best interests of its members were fully protected. That sounds a far cry from renationalisation without compensation, which was anyway missing from Labour's policy document for the 1983 General Election. That commits the Party simply to renationalisation, and on transport it only goes as far as aiming at *a* national freight company to control *a* publicly-owned share of the road-haulage industry.

The smallest of the four transport unions, the United Road Transport Union, was the most enthusiastic. Its General Secretary, Mr Jackson Moore, said that the executive committee regarded the consortium solution 'as an imaginative initiative and would wish it every success,' largely on the basis that 'the alternative is of course NO COMPANY.' The URTU came up with an imaginative idea of its own as well. Still quoting Mr Moore:

What is required now is for the staff to grasp the opportunity to buy shares (on the HP) and then to bring this Union in as the proxy for the employees to collectively look after the interests of all the workers in NFC.

But all the time the Consortium was dealing with union attitudes and their place in all the other aspects of communication it still had to keep its eye on the progress of the deal on the financial side: the banks too were finding their own difficulties.

5

ROLE OF THE BANKS

We couldn't contemplate financing this sort of exercise. (The buy-out). It was not our line of country.

> John Bushell, Director, J. Henry Schroder Wagg.

No independent merchant bank could have done it. They could not have underwritten the deal at the crucial time.

> Ron Watson, deputy managing director, Barclays Merchant Bank.

National Freight Consortium would not be in existence today had it not been for the support it received from the banks. But any suggestion that Barclays succeeded where Schroders failed would be well wide of the mark: certainly Barclays achieved a unique first in organising a comprehensive staff buy-out by harnessing the skills of the merchant banking arm to the financial muscle provided by its parent clearing bank, but Schroders, too, amply fulfilled its original brief. When Barclays started to act for the Consortium, Schroders continued to act for the Government and drove a hard bargain on final terms on its behalf.

In a sense banks can be likened to racehorses. Some horses

perform better on one racecourse than they do on another; some are at their best over sprints, while others with less speed but more stamina need longer distances to prove their mettle. It is these factors which have produced the phrase 'horses for courses', and that term can be applied with equal accuracy to different banks and types of banks.

The traditional merchant banks – the Rothschilds, Hambros and Barings of this world – trace their origins back to the eighteenth century when they were literally merchants turned bankers. The descendants of these pioneering banking families may be individually rich, but the banks themselves operate on a relatively small capital base. Their success is based on individual flair, flexibility to enable them to adapt quickly to changing circumstances, worldwide contacts which enable them to secure millions of pounds on the basis of a few phone calls (absolute mutual trust is essential to their business), and an inbuilt expertise in financial markets which, in many cases, has been built up over two centuries. Much of their income is derived from commissions and fees.

The major clearing banks – Barclays, Lloyds, NatWest and Midland – are in quite a different business. They are retail bankers with a large branch network, taking deposits from the general public, and making the bulk of their profits by re-lending this money at a higher rate of interest than they pay their depositors. This gives them control of massive assets, running into billions of pounds on which to base their lending. In simple terms, whereas a merchant bank will put together a loan package for a client, the clearing bank has the money available to lend from its 'own' resources – having already 'borrowed' it from its depositors.

Over the last dozen years the major clearers have built up (or in the case of Midland, bought) merchant banking facilities. This is partly because merchant banking is a lucrative occupation and partly because it was seen as a useful means of channelling banking business back to the parent bank. But early progress of the new merchant banks – Barclays Merchant

Bank and NatWest's County Bank – was slow: the traditional merchant banks were firmly entrenched, and their reputations extended world-wide. As we shall see, this background was to colour Barclays' attitude to the idea of an NFC Consortium solution.

When NFC appointed Schroders as financial advisers in the early summer of 1979, all that anyone had to go on was the Government's objectives as set out in its Election manifesto: 'The sale of shares in the NFC to the general public in order to achieve substantial private investment in it.' Schroders immediately began discussions with the Board and executive committee of NFC, and also with officials at the Department of Transport, and by July 23 was able to produce a paper 'Introduction of Private Investment into the NFC'. By this stage Schroders had seen NFC forecasts and plans from 1979 through to 1982, and had also had indications from the Government that if it (the Government) were to retain a shareholding it would only be a minority one, and that it would prefer NFC's business to remain substantially in its (then) present form.

On the basis of this somewhat nebulous information, Schroders prepared its assessment of the implications of an Offer for Sale of NFC shares to the public through the stock market (although other alternatives, such as a placing of shares with institutional investors and the sale of NFC minus its main loss makers were considered). One of the first points made by the bank was that it was, perforce, trying to project further into the future than was normal in any Offer for Sale: before the company could be brought to the market a new Transport Act would have to be passed, and then the business of the National Freight Corporation be passed to NFC Ltd. After that and the preparation of the prospectus based on 1980 results, a flotation could not be achieved before mid-1981 at the earliest, while at this stage the 1979 financial year was still far from over. Schroders admitted that its original estimate of around £60 million as a potential market value was hypothetical because of the numerous assumptions and caveats that had to be entered concerning NFC's actual performance against plan, the economic outlook, and the state of the stock market.

But at least Schroders had provided a 'ball park' figure for the valuation of NFC on a commercial basis, given that certain assumptions were met, and this figure could be adjusted subsequently to take into account any change in circumstances that occurred in the meantime. It also gave a basic timetable – although this too was subject to alteration depending on circumstances.

Schroders' observations and recommendations about changes that would be required in NFC's structure to make the nationalised business acceptable as a limited company were drawn up specifically with a Stock Exchange quotation in mind, but they laid the ground rules that were largely incorporated into NFC Ltd and subsequently NFC p.l.c. The first of these was that a commercial NFC should have a Board appropriate to a company listed on the Stock Exchange, and that implied a reasonable mix of executive and non-executive directors. The second major point related to pension deficiencies and other possible liabilities falling on NFC Ltd that would not fall on a normal quoted company, and the third to the treatment of NFC's capital debt to the Government, at that time £100 million: how much of that should be discharged and when?

On pensions, Schroders took the view that an Offer for Sale could not take place unless the Prospectus could state that the pension funds were adequately funded in respect of past liabilities, and that current contributions were at a level sufficient to cover benefits arising from current service: this effectively meant that the Government would have to fund the pension deficiencies to actuarial satisfaction. Later in its report Schroders commented:

any liability to compensate employees adversely affected by the transfer of ownership of the various parts of the business, either to NFC Ltd or on prior transfers, should remain with the Government.

On the question of the debt to the Government, and the whole capital structure of NFC Ltd, several possibilities were open. On the date that the Corporation became a limited company, all or part of the debt to the Government could be extinguished in exchange for equity held by the Secretary of State, and also the Appointed Day for that transition could be any time from the passing of the Act to a week before flotation.

These were tricky points, and were to give rise to a good deal of hard bargaining. Schroders took the view that the whole of the Government's £100 million should be written off in exchange for equity, largely due to NFC's high gearing. It pointed out that, because of low gross margins, NFC had a high level of 'operational' gearing in that a small change in the relationship between the level of cost and the level of income would have a disproportionate effect on profit levels, and also NFC had a high proportion of fixed costs – another gearing factor, since small changes in income are reflected in bigger changes in profits. Schroders also took into consideration that even if the past pension fund deficiencies were covered by the Government the Group was vulnerable to future deficiencies because the size of the pension funds would be large in relation to the group's equity capital and reserves. For these reasons the bank wanted to see NFC's capital structure geared as conservatively as possible, the more so because NFC had leasing obligations and other outside debt. There was also the point that cash limits on nationalised industries had restricted NFC's flexibility to develop and rationalise its business, and the smaller the debt burden that NFC Ltd inherited, the greater flexibility it would have to put this right.

On the question of the Appointed Day, Schroders said it would make little difference from the point of view of any Offer for Sale: the prospectus would simply show what past results would have been if calculated on the basis of the new capital structure. However, the bank agreed that, in management terms, it would be best for the Appointed Day to come as soon as possible after the Act was passed.

Schroders and the NFC Board campaigned long, hard and eventually victoriously on these issues in the face of opposition from the Treasury which preferred the certainty of interest payments on capital debt to a less certain dividend flow on an equity holding. Schroders looks on this as a victory for the 'broader view': that leaving the money within NFC put the company in a stronger position to carry on its business successfully.

The remainder of that Schroders paper is largely concerned with detailed aspects of a specific Offer for Sale which are therefore largely irrelevant now. But, significantly, on the basis of that original assessment, enough common ground was reached by the autumn of 1979 for the Department of Transport to invite the bank to advise both parties, and at the end of the day only two of Schroders' main points were not to be incorporated in the consortium solution. The first of these was the suggestion that NFC should be conservatively geared: but given the amount of loan finance required to make the consortium solution work, a high level of gearing was inevitable. Another condition that Schroders proposed was 'the transfer to NFC Ltd of all the benefits presently accruing to the NFC from handling the British Rail parcels business'. Ironically, it was the discontinuation of the BREPS service that put paid to any last chance of an Offer for Sale within a timescale acceptable to the Government, and paved the way for the Consortium – and Barclays – to take the stage. Schroders was not particularly dismayed by the turn of events:

> We felt perfectly happy about the way things turned out, [says John Bushell]. We knew that an Offer for Sale would have to be delayed, and that the Government would therefore be looking at alternative solutions. We had been working on this transaction for two years and were disap-

pointed by the prospect of a further indefinite period before the transaction could be completed. Consequently, the buy-out was an excellent solution for all those concerned.

Apart from its involvement in looking after the Government's interests, Schroders looks upon subsequent events fairly dispassionately.

Schroders admits that when the staff buy-out solution was mooted in early 1981 it did not think that Peter Thompson and his team had much chance of getting together a package that would give NFC people an 80 per cent equity stake. John Bushell comments:

> It is a great tribute to him, but also we had not taken into account the extent to which Barclays would be prepared to make available loan finance. We certainly would not have been prepared to put together that sort of loan package. It's not our type of banking. In a situation where clearing bank money is going to be a critical factor, then obviously the proposition is far better suited to someone like BMB than ourselves. It makes no difference to our own position in terms of our ability to offer corporate advice or in marketing securities.

The last point was amply justified by the success of the Associated British Ports Offer for Sale which Schroders later handled on behalf of the Government. The only fault critics could find there was that the offer was perhaps *too* successful, since the shares went to a substantial premium.

Anyway, as far as the Consortium was concerned, by April 1981 the ball was firmly in the court of Barclays Merchant Bank. It had to decide whether it was feasible to put together a package that would raise £52.5 million for the Consortium, but give NFC shareholders 80 per cent or more of the equity in return for less than 10 per cent of the total money raised. Schroders was right that BMB could, initially at least, look to the financial muscle of its parent bank for the loan finance required if the deal seemed right but first BMB had to convince itself, and then Barclays Bank, that the deal *was* right.

Even today Ron Watson smiles at the consternation in the NFC camp on that afternoon in April 1981 in Bedford when Barclays asked about the people and the business, and never once mentioned financial projections or security for loans.

'There is still a total misconception about modern banking', says Mr Watson. 'Of course the figures have got to be right, but they won't be right unless the business is right and the management is right.' BMB was aware that security for loans might be a problem under Section 54 of the 1948 Companies Act, although it underestimated the difficulties at that stage. However, viewing NFC as a 'special situation', it decided to tackle the problem from the other end: 'We started from the point of view that we wanted the management and staff of NFC to have control, and we would have to set out to find ways and means of achieving that end. On day one, neither we nor NFC knew if it was really possible', says Mr Watson.

As far as NFC was concerned, BMB decided to go ahead for a number of reasons. It felt that the management motivation was right and that the group was moving in the right direction. In view of the likely 1980 profit figures it was quite clear that a public Offer for Sale was not on, but Barclays took the view that NFC was composed of a mixture of dying businesses and growing businesses and, with nationalised industry restrictions removed from it, the group was moving as quickly as possible from the former to the latter. Closing obsolete businesses involves a lot of extraordinary costs which have to be absorbed, but at least they are one-off – while investment in growing businesses continues to pay dividends over time. Once Barclays had satisfied itself that the most difficult immediate problem – the reorganisation of the parcels division following the loss of the BREPS contract – was under control, the bank gave its confirmation, in principle, that it wanted to go ahead.

But NFC considerations were not the only things to be taken

into account. The NFC deal was a 'special situation' for
Barclays as well. It was a chance for the banking group as a
whole to show its paces.

Ron Watson happily admits that the NFC deal was a very
important one for BMB.

'In terms of publicity it was the biggest deal we had ever been
involved in. In retrospect, we probably had more publicity
over our involvement with NFC than in most of our other
deals put together. . . . [Pause] Thank goodness it went the
right way.'

It is impossible to judge just how heavily such considerations
weighed in the thinking of the Barclays group as a whole, but
under the original BMB proposal all the funds for what must be
classed at that stage as a risk project were to come from the
Barclays stable, and the bulk of the money was to be loan
finance. The outline terms for the (then) £45 million loan
stipulated that they should be secured against property worth
not less than £67.5 million, but at that stage in early June
no-one was quite sure how this security could be achieved
without breaching Section 54 of the 1948 Act. In theory
Barclays could have pulled out if no way had been found to get
round the problem; in practice it would have been hard for
them to do so, particularly after the joint NFC/BMB press
conference on June 18.

The first attempted solution to avoid Section 54 complications was to try to lend directly to fund the pension fund
deficiency, and then subsequently to secure that loan against
properties held within NFC Ltd. This could have been done if
the Government had laid down a Statutory Instrument putting
the onus of funding the pension deficiency on the company
rather than the Government. This could have been done under
Section 74 of the Transport Act 1967, but in this highly
technical area the Attorney General's Department advised the
Department of Transport that such a move would be 'uncon-

stitutional': although it may have been within the letter of the law, the Attorney General took the view that it offended against the spirit of the law.

NFC, Barclays, and other professional advisers looked for other means of cracking the Section 54 problem on security, but by the second week in August 1981 they threw in the towel in that respect, and it was here that Barclays took the biggest risk of all. Peter Thompson and his colleagues were getting edgy, because by now the whole workforce had been told about the buy-out – but behind closed doors it seemed to have come up against a brick wall. A new Companies Act was on its way that looked as if it should remove the Section 54 problems, but at that stage no-one could guarantee that it actually would. Barclays Merchant Bank felt that it had to do something if the deal was not to fall apart, took the bit between its teeth and asked its parent company to put up an unsecured loan of '£50 million plus'. All BMB could guarantee was that if the new Companies Act was favourable then security would be available, and on that basis the loan could then be syndicated to include other banks. If the Act in its final form did not solve the Section 54 problems, BMB could still try to syndicate the loan, but with a much smaller equity participation going to NFC people – at best 60 per cent instead of at least 80 per cent. Barclays Bank said yes, and Ron Watson is right in saying that no other merchant bank could or would have agreed to try and sell that sort of proposition at the critical moment.

That is by no means the end of BMB's involvement, but the rest belongs in subsequent chapters: particularly the next one which chronicles the mounting problems that still faced the consortium solution.

6

THE PROBLEMS MOUNT

500 staff meetings, 30 lawyers, 25 civil servants, 6 management briefings, 3 Queen's Counsel, 2 Secretaries of State, 1 Act of Parliament and 4 months later, I have come to realise that it wasn't quite as simple as I thought.

> Extract from a statement by Peter
> Thompson to the press following the
> announcement on October 17 1981 that the
> Government would sell NFC Ltd to an
> employee consortium.

Peter Thompson made those remarks almost four months to the day after the initial Press conference to announce the buy-out concept. Striking the quote may have been, but even so it does not tell the full story, and it could not take into account problems that were to arise subsequently. Reporting the events of October 17, internal NFC publications carried headlines such as: 'WE'VE DONE IT!' *'IT'S A DEAL'*; and 'Tremendous success for the consortium'. It is perhaps a good thing that the major 'WE'VE DONE IT!' headline in the October issue of NFC's *Management Bulletin* carried in brackets underneath, 'Well, nearly'. Because even after October 1981 there were many pitfalls to negotiate: the whole deal came within an ace of dying yet again in the week before Christmas, and even after the prospectus was published there was a nail-biting period when it looked as though NFC employees and pensioners were not going to subscribe for the minimum number of shares required of them for the deal to go through.

But returning to the summer of 1981, NFC and its advisers had to be active on many fronts. The decision by Barclays Bank to offer unsecured loan facilities allowed Peter Thompson to approach the Secretary of State for Transport, Norman Fowler, with a firm set of proposals for a staff buy-out – and Barclays Merchant Bank made it quite clear to the Consortium that it, and not BMB, would have to establish the limits of the price it was prepared to pay the Government: the eventual negotiations were undertaken by Michael Peterson of BMB on the Consortium's behalf and John Bushell of Schroders, representing the Department of Transport.

Even before that, however, first steps were being taken towards producing a prospectus for a consortium solution, and NFC was already reconciling itself to two possible routes to follow, either of which would secure the funds required to make the buy-out possible. Also, starting in August, regional and local presentations were being made to NFC's widely spread staff to explain the buy-out concept. A great deal of work went into these presentations, which themselves were fraught with difficulties: the workforce had to be persuaded to think of NFC as an entity, while most of them associated with their own subsidiary rather than the parent company; they had to be 'sold' an idea that was completely foreign to most of them, but great care had to be taken throughout to ensure that the Consortium did not stray into the realms of Prevention of Fraud Acts by 'pushing' shares, or offend against Companies Acts and Stock Exchange regulations in such areas as giving unauthorised profit forecasts. It is not surprising that Peter Thompson chafed under the restrictions placed on him by his legal and financial advisers, since none of the relevant rules had been drawn up with the unique NFC circumstances in mind.

Work actually began on the NFC prospectus on June 24,

when there was a meeting between NFC, BMB, solicitors Ashurst Morris Crisp and accountants Ernst & Whinney. This was even before detailed financing proposals had been discussed by the Consortium and BMB.

Although Barclays did not give its OK on unsecured lending until the second week in August, it was clear by the end of July – following meetings with Counsel and with the Government – that there were really only two workable solutions. The first relied on the 1981 Companies Act: (a) being passed in time to be of use to NFC, and (b) removing the Section 54 restrictions which prevented loans being secured against properties owned or leased by NFC subsidiaries. That was the preferred solution, since it would enable Barclays to put together a syndicate of banks which, because its loan finance was secured, would settle for around 20 per cent of the equity of the new NFC and leave 80 per cent or more for those participating in the staff buy-out.

The fall-back solution which would be used if the Companies Act option was not available was much less satisfactory, and much more complicated. Called the 'ring fence' alternative, it involved unsecured lending by a banking syndicate which, in return, would expect a much higher level of equity participation – leaving NFC members with between 50 per cent and 60 per cent of the equity: still in control, but not so convincingly.

In simple terms this scheme rested on the fact that there were a lot of interest-free unsecured inter-company loans within the NFC group, which could gradually be converted into loans made on a commercial basis – bearing interest and secured against property assets. This is how the ring fence solution would have worked: the banks would lend the £50 million plus to 'NEWCO' (the Consortium) secured against its only asset – its 100 per cent shareholding in NFC Ltd. On day one that would effectively have been an unsecured loan, since NFC Ltd was itself a holding company for the trading subsidiaries. However, as loans fell due for repayment, or were called in, they would be re-negotiated on a commercial basis so that NFC Ltd would receive both interest and security against property assets. Gradually therefore, NFC Ltd – and so NEWCO – would have shares with a real asset value, and the banks' unsecured loans would increasingly become secured.

Although everything turned out right in the end, the ring fence option plays a very important part in the overall story. In September 1981, before the new Companies Bill became law, Barclays had to syndicate a double-edged package: solution 1 (via the Companies Act) would not be a problem, but at that stage there was still a real possibility that the syndicating banks would have to settle for solution 2 (the 'ring fence'), which was a far less attractive banking proposition. It says a lot for BMB's powers of persuasion that it got NatWest, its merchant banking subsidiary County Bank, Lloyds Bank and Williams and Glyns to accept this double-edged sword, as well as its own parent. Finance For Industry (FFI) was also involved in the early stages. It decided to pull out and rather than invite someone else the remaining partners absorbed the FFI share *pro rata*.

Between the beginning of August and Christmas 1981 there was an incredible amount of activity, and to chronicle all the meetings that took place during those five months would require an encyclopaedia rather than a book. However, to give a flavour of what went on during that period here are just some of the things that were going on and some of the problems that had to be resolved:

The Consortium had to negotiate a fair price for NFC with the Government, which by this stage was being advised by Schroders. NFC's Chairman, Sir Robert Lawrence, who had got clearance from the Secretary of State for the buy-out idea to be explored, had effected the introduction of the Consortium to BMB, and had spearheaded discussion with the unions was now, 'holding the ring' to look after the company's interests (effectively the Government's).

The final price could not be struck until agreement had been reached between the Government Actuary and NFC's own actuaries on the exact pension fund deficiency. Victor Paige, as chairman of the Pension Fund, was actively involved in these negotiations, as was John Ager, NFC's Chief Pensions Officer.

The Consortium and Barclays had to work out detailed financial terms for the two possible routes to a buy-out.

The Consortium and BMB had to persuade the proposed banking syndicate to accept the two possible deals, and a whole-day presentation took place at Bedford on October 1.

Almost 1,000 NFC properties had to be sifted to choose those which would be used to secure loans if the first solution proved to be available.

Profit forecasts or expectations had to be produced and subsequently looked at by the auditors.

Throughout the whole period work was going on to prepare the prospectus. This was a mammoth and complex task, and the final prospectus emerged only after an unprecedented 49 proofs.

The Consortium had to carry out an almost continuous campaign to explain the idea of the buy-out to NFC employees and, as time went on, to keep them up to date with progress and maintain the enthusiasm.

The Consortium, Barclays and the Department of Transport had to be in close touch with the Department of Trade: the Companies Bill had not been drawn up for NFC's benefit, but it was of paramount importance that the detailed working of key clauses should be unambiguous where they could affect NFC's special case.

Means had to be found to draw up an employee loan scheme that would not offend against any of the Companies Acts.

A mechanism had to be devised for valuing NFC's shares since there would be no open-market valuation, and rules had to be worked out for trading in the shares once they were issued.

While all this was going on, NFC's executive directors and senior managers, many of whom were directly involved in the Consortium, still had to find time for their primary job: the management of NFC on a day-to-day basis.

That list is by no means exhaustive (although definitely exhausting to those involved) and it goes some way to explaining Peter Thompson's catalogue of meetings and so forth which only takes the subject up to the middle of October. It was a frenetic time for everyone concerned, and particularly for members of the Consortium who had to be involved in, or informed of, everything that went on.

The degree of complexity involved can, perhaps, be measured by the fact that property, pensions, the prospectus, and staff communications each rate a chapter of the book to themselves – and that is with the benefit of hindsight. Ron Watson of BMB still has a harried look about him when he recalls those months, and Peter Thompson is probably only half joking when he says with a smile: 'If we had known what we were letting ourselves in for I doubt if we'd have even tried it'. Certainly candles were burnt at both ends in many offices, in some meetings emotions ran high and tempers frayed and, as often as not, elation at a problem solved was quickly tempered by deflation when two other difficulties emerged to fill the gap.

It would be nice to give a well-ordered account of those five hectic months; to say there was a crucial decision 'A' that led to subsequent decisions 'B', 'C', 'D' etc., but it just did not work out that way. Virtually no meeting was definitive: no matter how much the parties agreed round one table, the decision taken was hedged with safeguarding clauses concerning related issues that were being discussed elsewhere. In retrospect everything looks fairly neat and tidy but in fact there was a certain amount of chaos. By this stage over a hundred people –

all highly qualified in their respective fields – were involved, but they were trying to break new ground. Worse still, that new ground had large patches of quicksand because of the unknown quantity of the 1981 Companies Act.

At this time BMB was perhaps most in the firing line since it had to sell the concept of financing the consortium (including the 'ring fence' route) to the other banks. On September 28 it produced a document of 22 pages (twice that if Appendices are taken into account) which laid down the ground rules for the two potential solutions, went into considerable detail about NFC's achievements and aspirations and asked for three things: a medium-term banking facility of £51 million, a trading facility of around £30 million, and an equity participation of between 15 per cent and 40 per cent depending on which of the two options was to be followed.

It was, of course, a highly professional document which went into considerable detail about assets, dividend cover on the proposed dividend policy, profit forecasts, and all the other things that bankers like to know before they lend money. It had only one drawback: it turned out to be too ambitious in profit terms, mainly due to the continuation of the economic recession.

The original Barclays' figures were drawn up on the basis of NFC projections, but as those figures were being circulated – in the autumn of 1981 – NFC's management was revising profit forecasts in the light of the current economic scene, with each Group submitting figures to the centre about the likely outcome for the following calendar year. James Watson counselled for achievable, conservative forecasts, and the Board had several hard talking meetings to agree the final financial profit forecasts. After a final Board meeting on December 13, the lower forecasts were sent to Barclays, who were obviously concerned. Then a series of difficult meetings ensued, but there was no escaping the fact that the new figures would have to go to the syndicate banks.

The revised forecasts, perhaps more than anything else at

that time, brought the deal to the brink of disaster since the syndicate banks were none too pleased at having to accept downgraded estimates. They were, however, satisfied by Barclays, partly because unknown to NFC, on September 28 Barclays had circulated the Banks with a 30-page assessment of NFC's profit forecasts outlining the areas of risk and suggesting that they were possibly optimistic and would not be achieved, particularly if the economic recession continued. Ron Watson of BMB recalls emphasising to Peter Thompson and James Watson the need to 'make sure that you get your forecasts right this time, because we can't go back to the syndicate a third time'.

Throughout this trying period everyone was still looking over their shoulders at the 1981 Companies Act. The Act did not receive Royal Assent until October 30, and even then Commencement Orders had to be laid to bring its provisions into force. The first of these was published on November 18 to take effect from December 3, bringing Sections 42–4 of the Act into effect. These were the most crucial of the provisions of the Act as far as NFC was concerned, since they got the Consortium and its supporters off the hook of the Section 54 provisions of the 1948 Act. It was not pure accident that these were the first sections of the Act to be introduced: A Department of Trade press release on November 18 specifically pointed out that their introduction would make buy-outs such as the Consortium was attempting much easier to achieve.

Although Section 42 of the new Act broadly restated the prohibitions of the old Section 54, the two succeeding sections – 43 and 44 – provided a route whereby a private company such as the National Freight Company could now legally give financial assistance in the purchasing of its shares. The way through the legislation for the Consortium imposed yet another onerous obligation for the directors of National Freight Company and most of its subsidiaries, all of whom had to make statutory declarations, and involved a series of undertakings about debts and liabilities, plus an auditor's report for each company concerned. (An alternative, and rather less tiresome, path was provided by the new Act – for cases where financial assistance was part of a larger plan for the company – but after examination, and not a little legal argument, it was decided that this could not be prayed in aid of the Consortium's situation.)

This solved NFC's overwhelming problem in that the new rules allowed loans from the banks to be secured against properties which were legally held by subsidiaries of the parent holding company. Unfortunately it also created a few new problems: the onus for making such decisions was left with the directors of the operating companies, not the parent company, and therefore every subsidiary had to decide what it could remit to the parent company and which properties it could allow to be mortgaged – in each case staying within the letter of the law as laid down by the new, untried, Act. Needless to say, a lot of hastily convened Board meetings followed.

It all sounds very cumbersome, and indeed it was. But if you are a director of a company you break any provisions of any Companies Act at your own personal peril: the law may be an ass sometimes, but it still has to be obeyed. And under the law ignorance of it is no excuse.

This was not the only thing that conspired against a quick solution. Schroders, acting for the Government, refused to negotiate a final price for NFC until the actuaries had agreed on the pension deficiency, and the price of £53.5 million agreed in October 1981 was therefore subject to final agreement of the pensions funding. Also, it was not until late in November that agreement was reached on property valuation for the loan security for the banks. Then, it was well into December before the Consortium's downward profit revisions were received and, after much discussion, the amended forecasts submitted to the syndicate of banks. It was to go to the day before Christmas Eve until the last 'i' was dotted and the last 't' crossed on the loan package: the medium term loan agreement had already been finalised, but it was not until December 24 that the short term finance was agreed.

It is doubtful whether anyone who was not involved in those various negotiations will ever understand the strain that it imposed on those who were involved. For example, who would pay if everything went wrong: would it be the Department of Transport, would it be Barclays, or would it be the members of the Consortium who, in their private capacity, would have been hard pushed at best to get together the money to meet a bill that was already amounting to hundreds of thousands of pounds? Before the eventual solution was achieved the Government's view was that it should bear only 'normal' costs; for a while the new company was a subsidiary of Barclays Bank, which had provided the minimum initial capital required to set up a public company, and the Consortium was feeling distinctly uncomfortable – because there was a real possibility that the tab would be laid at its door. These are the sort of considerations that everyone tends to forget after the event – when everything has turned out to be all right.

Until the Consortium's Offer for Sale was safely oversubscribed by 3 p.m. on February 16 1982 a whole lot of things could have gone wrong. As this chapter has indicated, the deal could have foundered on any number of counts and it really is difficult to put them in any sort of order of precedence. If, for example, NFC people had not subscribed for enough shares at the end of the day then all the hard work that had gone into the Consortium idea would have been wasted. In terms of big numbers, however, the idea could never have got off the ground in the first place if the problem of the pension fund deficiency had not been resolved to everyone's (more or less) satisfaction. And that has a chapter to itself.

7

THE GOVERNMENT'S POSITION

One justification of Shadow Ministers in Opposition is that it gives them time to study problems they may eventually have to deal with in Office.

> Quote from an interview with Norman Fowler, Minister and then Secretary of State for Transport through most of the denationalisation and staff buy-out negotiations.

When looking at the NFC buy-out, the most obvious question to ask is why it became a political *cause célèbre* in the first place. After all, a Conservative Party committed to returning as much of British nationalised industries to the private sector as possible had much larger fish to fry than a £50 million company that – although the biggest single company in the road haulage industry – still controlled not much more than 7 per cent of the market. As events have subsequently proved, there were organisations at least 10 times that size which had far more commanding market shares in other areas of the public sector and which could be sold off.

Norman Fowler, at the time of writing Secretary of State for Health and Social Security, is the best man to answer that question since, in the early days at least, it was purely a matter of party politics: and it was Mr Fowler who, as Shadow Transport Minister, wrote the Conservative Party pamphlet on transport, 'The Right Track' back in 1977 – and, unusually, in such exercises, wrote every word of it himself. Asked why he produced that document when he did, Mr Fowler replied with a statement of masterly political pragmatism:

> Well, the Labour Party had published the Crosland 'Orange Document' on Transport and I felt that the Tories needed to reply. It struck me that we hadn't had many pamphlets on Transport policy from our side.

But why, then, the specific reference to NFC?

> I came to the conclusion that NFC was a good business trying to get out. There was no logical reason for it to be in the public sector: indeed there was no logical reason for the NFC at all: very few people outside of those directly involved were even aware of NFC's existence. People identified with the operating subsidiaries, but not with the parent Corporation.

Mr Fowler stresses that the early Conservative attitudes on Transport were his own. 'It was not a major issue in the House of Commons and neither was it a major consideration within the Party', he said, and this goes some way towards explaining later discrepancies between the Government view as expressed by Mr Fowler, and the NFC fears that unacceptable solutions might be considered to expedite hiving off all or part of the Corporation within a given time scale. According to Mr Fowler, although NFC was specifically mentioned in the 1979 election manifesto as a candidate for privatisation, there was no real political pressure on him from his Cabinet colleagues to achieve that aim within a particular period: 'I just wanted to finish the job', he commented.

Asked why there had been no specific reference to NFC in the Queen's Speech setting out proposed Government legislation Mr Fowler replied that the speech implied the inclusion of NFC on its privatisation list.

> The Queen's Speech is not an occasion for spelling out the legislative programme chapter and verse. The Speech did say 'other proposals will reduce the extent of nationalised and state ownership and increase competition by providing offers of sale including offers for employees to participate, where appropriate'. That was intended to cover NFC.

Norman Fowler's recollection of reactions within NFC when the idea was first mooted is interesting. NFC recollections are that the idea of being released from nationalised industry shackles such as cash limits was quickly welcomed; Mr Fowler remembers that some top people at the Corporation took some convincing that the idea of the change was a good one.

> There was general acceptance that joint projects with private sector companies might be a good idea, but there still existed within NFC (though not throughout it) a nationalised industry mentality that questioned the necessity of a total change in status.

Nevertheless, when the Conservatives came into power Mr Fowler became first Minister and then Secretary of State for Transport, and within his own Department he made it clear that the privatisation of NFC was a priority: on his arrival, one of the first things he asked his Civil Servants for was action and advice on transferring all or part of NFC to the private sector, and this therefore became a priority for the staff of the Department.

The four senior men most involved throughout were Sir

Peter Baldwin, the Permanent Secretary, Mr Peter Lazarus, Deputy Secretary, Transport Industries, Mr Giles Hopkinson, Under Secretary, Freight, and Mr Patrick Brown, Assistant Secretary, Finance. In terms of the eventual Consortium solution Sir Peter Baldwin operated at the strategic level, lending his support to exploration of the consortium idea at the outset, and signing the deal on behalf of the Government when terms had been finally agreed, while Peter Lazarus led the Government's side in negotiations at Board level which brought about the eventual agreement. The bulk of the detailed discussion at working party level was headed on the Government's side by Giles Hopkinson, with Patrick Brown particularly involved in sorting out the financial nitty gritty.

But long before the Consortium came along the senior Civil Servants were heavily involved in planning the best route to achieve what one of them described as the Government's 'vague promise'.

Governments, Ministers, and their advisers are subject to quite different pressures, political and otherwise, from those imposed on private and even nationalised industries. All three are subject to intensive lobbying by incompatible pressure groups, and any government has to allocate scarce Parliamentary time and draw up a list of priorities from a host of legislative proposals, all of which cannot possibly be achieved in the time available. Within the cabinet, Ministers fight fiercely for a share of that Parliamentary time to push through their own pet projects, as well as trying to make sure that their own Departments interpret their ideas correctly into firm policies. The Departments have to try to accede to their Minister's wishes, guide him where necessary, and also make sure that Parliamentary draughtsmen draw up proposed legislation in such a form that an eventual Act will be interpreted as saying exactly what it is meant to say. All three groups are almost perpetually at loggerheads with the Treasury, part of whose duty it sees as being as parsimonious as possible, and Civil Servants have the added threat of ac-

countability to the Public Accounts Committee – the House of
Commons watchdog on the use of public money.

All these factors played a part in the Government's approach
to privatising NFC. In the normal meetings that are usual
between new Ministers and their senior departmental advisers
Mr Fowler and his senior Civil Servants decided that an Offer
for Sale through the stock market was the preferable solution.

Shortly after the Minister was appointed therefore it became
clear that Parliamentary time would have to be found for a
Transport Bill that could make this route feasible. The Freight
and Finance Directorates were given the task of working out
between them, and in consultation with the Treasury, the final
shape that the new NFC should take, and what monetary terms
would be agreeable to the Government.

The Department did not work in a vacuum: there was
considerable contact between Civil Servants and the NFC both
officially and unofficially at all levels, and it quickly became
clear that there was much common ground between the views
of the Transport officials and those of the NFC. The Department therefore set up right at the outset a joint working party
composed of members of its Policy and Finance directorates,
NFC, Schroders and solicitors Freshfields. As one Department
spokesman put it: 'It was a team with one common aim –
privatisation'. The inclusion of Schroders in that team was to
lead to it acting formally for both NFC and the Government
which, in turn, was to have considerable political ramifications.
The purpose of this powerful team was both to ensure that the
Transport Bill covered all the relevant technical details and
that it also accurately represented the intentions of the
consensus – and there was an added plus that Victor Paige, a
key figure from the NFC side, and Giles Hopkinson, already
knew each other very well – thus assisting a feeling of mutual
confidence.

By appointing Schroders to act as joint advisers the Department of Transport had implicitly accepted the main Schroders'
recommendations and observations made in its original as-

sessment when it was working for NFC alone. Not only did it commit the Government to a specific price range on an Offer for Sale (on the facts and figures then available) – it also implied the Government's acceptance of two other major points. The first of these was that no public sale would be possible without the pension fund deficit being funded, and the second that NFC should not be encumbered with any liabilities outside of those which would be incumbent on any other public company.

On the question of pensions, it was already clear that the only acceptable political solution was for the Government to fund the deficit out of the proceeds of the sale of the company, and it would not be possible to do this if only a small proportion – or even a small majority – of the shares were sold off.

The Minister knew therefore that to achieve his preferred solution of an Offer for Sale he was committed to the sale of most or all of NFC, and, for the same reason, he could not saddle a publicly quoted NFC with any safeguards to the unions about conditions of employment for the workforce of the group. Both these points were hotly contested by the unions involved. On August 22 1979 the Department had circulated the relevant unions with a policy document outlining the Government's proposals, and on September 26 there was a meeting with union representatives where they pressed for the Government to retain at least a 50 per cent stake in NFC, and also for the 'no-worsening' clause. On the first point Mr Fowler stood firm: he would make no commitment, but the Government intended to sell a 'substantial proportion' of NFC to the public. On the second point the Government was prepared to agree up until the time of the Offer for Sale, but after that it was a matter for free collective bargaining outside the State system. The Government again came under heavy pressure on both these points when the Transport Bill reached Committee stage, but again it remained firm, and the Bill came back down to the floor of the House substantially unchanged.

As has been pointed out earlier, just as the Transport Act was receiving Royal Assent, NFC's fortunes took a turn for the worse, and after the Appointed Day, when the Company took over from the Corporation, that trend continued. The NFC and its advisers had won a rare victory over the Treasury to get Mr Fowler to nominate the Appointed Day sooner rather than later, but then Department officials had to advise the Minister that in view of the changed circumstances there was no possibility of an early flotation. At that stage it looked as though the Minister had swapped fixed interest loans of £100 million for equity of questionable value.

With public accountability in mind, the Government had to start thinking in vague terms at least about alternative solutions to the Offer for Sale route, and during February and March Mr Fowler (who had become Secretary of State for Transport in January) was instructing his Department to investigate such possibilities. A tender offer *à la* Thomas Cook had already been rejected, but general consideration was still being given to investigating the idea of a single purchase solution. Apart from anything else 'an oblique approach' had been received from a Swiss merchant bank – although this subsequently came to nothing.

It was against this background that Sir Robert Lawrence approached the Secretary of State on April 9 to sound him out on the possibility of a buy-out by a management-led consortium, and received a favourable response from Mr Fowler to pursue the idea further. However, Mr Fowler does not subscribe to the popularly held view that the Consortium got himself and the Government 'off the hook'. According to the Secretary of State:

> It wasn't really like that, although it was a good potential solution as far as the Government was concerned. The Government's initial job had been to pass legislation that would enable NFC to be transferred to the private sector, but it could still have gone a number of ways. The real political decision was to find the way through that would be good for the NFC and good for the Government.

In May the Consortium put an outline proposal to Mr Fowler which, according to Peter Thompson, was given 'a warm welcome', and at this point the Consortium wanted this to be the only proposal on the table. This desire was understandable, since it would have removed a major element of uncertainty from the Consortium's point of view when selling the idea to NFC employees. But the Department said it would not, and indeed could not, accept that condition: it had to be seen to get the best terms possible for the sale of NFC, and therefore had to allow the opportunity for other, more attractive offers unless it wanted the Public Accounts Committee breathing down its neck.

This was the reason for the public statement by the Secretary of State on June 18 announcing his welcome for the Consortium's proposals – and the Consortium/BMB Press conference was timed to coincide with that announcement. In fact between June 18 and the completion of the deal on October 17 (when Sir Peter Baldwin and Peter Thompson initialled the agreement), the Department did have another approach but this, like the Swiss bank initiative, came to nothing.

In a situation of potential conflict like this, it was of the greatest importance to the Government to get clearly independent financial advice so that it could be seen to be separating the political and financial dimensions of the case. Shortly after the June announcement, therefore, Schroders, at the Department's insistence, became advisers solely to the Government.

The negotiation of the terms between the Government and the Consortium was left largely in the hands of the two merchant banks, BMB and Schroders and – since the sums rested almost solely on an agreement on the pension fund deficiencies – on the Government Actuary and actuaries working for the Consortium. But once the signatures were on the dotted line the ball was firmly in the Consortium's court to deliver the goods to complete the deal.

Almost up to the date of signing the agreement the final Government decisions had rested with Mr Fowler, but about a

A happy Peter Thompson watches Sir Peter Baldwin, Permanent Secretary at the Department of Transport, initialling the provisional agreement to sell the NFC to the consortium. An event witnessed by senior NFC managers on Saturday October 17 1981 at a meeting in Bedford.

week beforehand he moved on to be Secretary of State for Health, and from that point onwards the final arbiter on the Government side was the new Transport Secretary Mr David Howell who, at the end of the day, accepted the Consortium's £53.5 million cheque on behalf of the Government.

8

SORTING OUT THE PENSIONS

More than £47 million of the money which the Secretary of State received for NFC will be paid to the NFC Pension Funds. The Government will also continue to provide some other financial support for the Funds.

Extract from NFC p.l.c. Prospectus, Appendix 9.

It is doubtful that even a dozen people understand all the implications of NFC's pension problems. On top of the historical problems – some British Rail employees are in NFC funds and vice-versa – there were actuarial (i.e. valuation) and political problems to be solved at the time of the buy-out. There is no denying that the details are technical, but equally there is no denying just how important they were: the Government gave back more than 80 per cent of the £53.5 million it was paid for NFC to put the pension funds back onto a footing that would be acceptable in a normal commercial enterprise – where there is no automatic government guarantee to make good any shortfall in the pension fund and so the company itself has to transfer money to guaranteed pension funds.

Pension fund deficiencies can arise in a number of ways. In an ideal world pension fund contributions paid in by employees together with the contributions paid by employers should be invested and when the employee retires the accumulated sum should provide enough to meet his guaranteed pension. In the real world however things tend to work out rather differently.

Pensions are usually based on a proportion of final salary, that proportion depending on the terms of the scheme, and the length of service which an employee has with the company. However in periods of rising incomes an employee's salary on retirement entitles him to a pension which is in excess of the sum of the contributions invested for him/her over the years. Also, as acceptable social standards are raised over time there is a tendency for the terms offered by pension funds to improve, but the amounts charged to existing contributors to a scheme cannot be backdated to take into account the improved benefits now being offered. A third major force comes into effect when pension funds are index-linked – that is payments to pensioners rise automatically in line with, or as a proportion of, the increase in the retail price index.

The net effect of this is that gradually pensions come to be paid not from the contributions made by the pensioner in the past, but from higher pension contributions being made by those who are currently employed. The state pension scheme has been forced to operate on this pay-as-you-go basis for years.

This however is only part of the story. Although companies are obliged to ensure that their pension schemes have adequate funds to meet their pension obligations, they have no control whatsoever over the valuation or running of the pension funds, which is handled by a totally independent body of pension fund trustees who, in turn, employ highly qualified actuaries and investment managers. The job of the investment manager is to make the best return possible on the money held by the pension fund, while the actuary has to decide whether the fund has enough resources to meet its present *and future* liabilities. He makes these calculations on more or less established facts, e.g. the number of people due to retire in any given year, and informed guesses as to the likely movements in inflation, salaries and rates of interest. To the extent that a fund cannot cover its present and future liabilities for existing members and pensioners there is a pension fund deficiency.

Actuarial assessments for pension funds will vary depending on the assumptions and forecasts used by the actuaries involved. In the case of NFC the picture is made considerably more complex because it has three funds – one for salaried staff, one for wages grade staff, a smaller NFC (1978) Pension Fund and also a small number of employees who elected to stay with British Rail pension schemes although their employers became NFC under the 1968 Transport Act.

The cross membership of pension funds dates back to the 1948 Transport Act and all subsequent Transport Acts which have included the provision that people moving jobs within the nationalised transport sector are not obliged to move from one pension fund to another, and when control of National Carriers and Freightliners was shifted from British Rail to NFC in 1969 following the 1968 Transport Act one third of the NFC workforce, or around 15,000 people, were ex-BR employees. In 1971 NFC set up a new pensions funds structure and many ex-BR employees took advantage of the offer of shifting from BR pension funds to the relevant NFC pension fund, while others took advantage of similar opportunities extended in 1975 and 1978.

In 1978, when NFC had its capital reconstruction, alterations were made to the pension funds as well. The government agreed to fund the deficit for the rail-based employees, but not for the road-based employees. It reimbursed NFC itself for some of the payments it had made to the funds under arrangements similar to those introduced for BRB under the 1974 Railways Act. Since rail-based and road-based employees were now all lumped together within the two main NFC funds, the actuaries had to apportion which parts of the two funds related to rail-based employees and therefore the extent of government funding required.

This gives a (simplified!) background to the situation in which NFC found itself in relation to pension obligations prior to the 1980 Transport Act. Bearing in mind that the primary aim of that Act was to allow the re-creation of NFC in a form that would be acceptable for a stock market flotation, it was obvious that the pensions situation had to be clearly spelt out, and would have to satisfy the City that NFC was not being left with an unacceptable pensions burden.

At that time more than 95 per cent of eligible employees were members of the two main NFC funds set up in 1971, and by the time the Prospectus was published there were 25,000 people contributing to the two schemes, and 14,000 pensioners drawing from them. In September 1981 the value of the assets of the funds was more than £155 million.

The solution adopted in the 1980 Act basically allowed for a four-way split. Each of the two categories of pension liabilities in the funds – rail-based and road-based – were to be split into two sub-groups, 'historic' and 'non-historic'. Historic obligations are defined as those which were entered into before April 1 1975, and the Government would meet any shortfall arising out of liabilities incurred before that date. These historic obligations basically arise from the guarantee by the employers of benefits for periods of past-service credited membership granted to employees joining the main Funds from previous schemes. In the case of the smaller NFC (1978) Pension Fund, which had been unfunded and which consists almost entirely of pensioners, the historic obligations cover all of the pensions paid. The method to be adopted however varied between the two main categories of members. In the case of the road-based employees, the Government would hand over a lump sum to cover unfunded liabilities once and for all, but with the rail-based employees it decided to change the method of meeting the unfunded liabilities by paying them as they arose, month by month. The main reason for this was that under a separate part of the Act, revised arrangements for supporting the British Rail Pension Funds were set out, and the rail-based NFC Fund obligations were to be treated in the same way.

Effectively therefore, any historic rail-based deficiencies will continue to be met by the Government as they have been in the past, and this was confirmed to the Consortium by David Howell in a letter to Peter Thompson dated October 26 1981. The funding also applies to comparable NFC obligations to its employees in funds run by the British Railways Board.

But for the road-based obligations the arrangement was quite different. Once the lump sum payment had been made all future unfunded liabilities of the Consortium pension funds were to be the responsibility of the Consortium, but here again there are a couple of caveats that have to be entered. In the first place the NFC pension funds are index linked in line with increases granted to public service pensioners, and the payments by Government allowed for increases in the historic element of pension benefits up to the level of pension increases granted to retired public servants. The Government therefore has recognised responsibility for the historic part of the index-linking of NFC pensions, although it is not responsible for any improvements in the pension schemes introduced by NFC since 1975 or in the future.

The other point to note is that if there is a shortfall in the pension funds arising from the non-historic part of the liabilities, then NFC is not *obliged* to make up this shortfall. Should such a shortfall occur it would be met by an adjustment of relevant benefits, unless it was agreed that one or both of the parties involved – the employers and the employees – should pay additional contributions.

Given all this, the main point at issue was just what the lump sum payment should be in respect of historic non-rail liabilities. The Act stipulated that the sum would be determined by the Secretary of State and in practice he would act on the advice of the Government Actuary.

That sounds straightforward enough, but it must be remembered that the unfunded obligations incurred up to the end of 1975 included future liabilities for people in the pension schemes who might not be drawing their pensions for another 30 years or more. Therefore the actuaries were not simply adding up a known historic liability, but projecting figures well into the future. This they did on the basis of past experience and assumptions about future economic expectations.

Although the final word lay with the Secretary of State, NFC was not just standing on the sidelines waiting for the oracle to speak. It had its own team of actuaries working out projections – and therefore the Government's immediate liability – and not surprisingly the figures they came up with differed markedly from those produced by the Government Actuary. The main area of disagreement was on economic forecasts, with the Government Actuary leaning far more towards the Government's own optimistic economic predictions than NFC was prepared to do. Some hard bargaining followed, and although the Government was not prepared to budge on the longer term assessment used by the Government Actuary it did adjust the short term predictions to give weight to the then current scene.

NFC's Chief Pensions Officer John Ager says that in the bargaining which followed NFC achieved 'a significant improvement in terms'. NFC did not achieve all it wanted because at the end of the day Civil Servants negotiating were the accounting officers as far as the Public Accounts Committee was concerned, and therefore had to pay due regard to the advice of the Government Actuary.

Right from the start Mr Ager, and Victor Paige as chairman of the Pension Funds Trustees had stood apart from the Consortium in respect of the Pension Fund negotiations. As Mr Ager put it

> right from day one when I heard about the Consortium I took the view that if people were to risk losing life savings by joining the Consortium they were certainly not going to lose their pension rights. I was therefore determined that nothing should happen which could violate the security of the pension funds.

The final agreed road-based liability was £47,297,000 which

the Government paid into the funds almost as soon as the Consortium handed over its cheque for £53.5 million to the Secretary of State. The actuary to the pension funds advised the trustees that this fell £2 million short of the actual obligations in his view, but this shortfall was considered acceptable. (Subsequently 'relatively small' adjustments resulted in a further payment of £1.3 million by the Government, so that at the end of the day the Government actually sold the NFC equity for just £5 million in cash.)

This solution left NFC with all its pension liabilities funded with the exception of an estimated shortfall not exceeding £10 million in the Salaried Staff Fund. The trustees were happy as long as this was met in an appropriate manner, in accordance with the terms of the Trust Deeds and Rules of this Fund, and in the opinion of the Directors of the Consortium, any costs in this connection were within the financial capacity of the Consortium and the member companies of the NFC Group.

Moving away from the financial side of the pension scene, there was one other problem to be solved in relation to pensioners, and this was – just who would be eligible to apply for shares in the Consortium.

In spite of legal problems which had to be overcome it was decided that pensioners in receipt of pensions together with their husbands or wives should be included – after all it would be an arbitrary line to draw between someone who was to retire in a week's time, and someone who had retired just a week ago. There was also the genuine feeling that NFC pensioners were as much 'a part of the family' as those still actively employed within the group, and in addition to this moral approach there was the practical advantage that the catchment area of potential shareholders was widened by more than 50 per cent. In the end the Consortium had reason to be pleased with its decision, since some 1,300 pensioners applied for shares when the time came.

9

PROPERTY COMPLICATIONS

The medium term loan will be secured by joint and several guarantees from NFC and its major subsidiaries. In the majority of cases, these guarantees will also be secured by first legal charges over freehold and leasehold properties owned by the guarantors.

> Extract from the security provisions covering the medium term loan to NFC from the banking syndicate.

That guarantee clause securing loans against a first mortgage on properties owned by the borrower is standard practice. In principle it is not very different from a building society mortgage on a house where the society can take possession of the property if the purchaser fails to keep up with his mortgage repayments. But it will come as no surprise that the property negotiations involved in the Consortium's dealings with the banking syndicate were every bit as complicated as any other part of the whole story.

As soon as it was obvious that the 1981 Companies Act would allow the banks' medium term loans to be secured directly by mortgages on properties held by NFC subsidiaries it was equally clear that this would be the route that would be taken: it was the original 'preferred solution'. The fact that the security had to be obtained from each individual subsidiary company under the terms of the Act rather than through a single deal with the parent company was a tiresome administrative burden, but that really was the least of the problems in finding properties within the NFC portfolio that would be regarded as suitable security for a medium term loan of £51 million.

The deal which Barclays Merchant Bank had set up with the other members of the banking syndicate was that the £51 million medium term loan would be covered by a first charge on properties worth approximately one and a half times that amount. This was not such a conservative move on the part of the banks as it might appear, since they were also making available to the Consortium a trading facility of £30 million. If the worst came to the worst therefore the banks were in for £81 million against security of £76.5 million.

But there were a number of snags involved in arriving at this level of security. The first was the sheer size and diversity of the NFC property portfolio: not only did it have 700 trading locations, the total number of properties involved was in excess of 1,000. Some of these were large and obviously valuable while others were small and relatively insignificant, but it would obviously have been impossible to carry out a thorough investigation of the whole property portfolio. At the end of the day some 250 property sites were included in the security package, but within the timescale of the whole operation it was not physically possible to do comprehensive valuations and title searches on all of these.

Title searches were another major headache. Many properties were transferred to National Freight Corporation from British Rail under the 1968 Transport Act via National Carriers, but in terms of the property world this shift did not necessarily represent a satisfactory succession of title as far as the properties were concerned. There were also many other complications concerning rights of way and suchlike which were perhaps of little consequence to NFC, but which could have had a considerable impact on the market value of the land concerned. The third major headache lay in the fact that NFC valued its properties on what is called existing use value, while people looking to charge properties in order to secure loans are much more concerned with what the land and buildings are worth on the open market.

The two people chiefly involved on the property valuation side were Alan Butterfield, NFC's chief surveyor, and Terry Tindall of Barclays Merchant Bank. Also tied into that side of affairs was NFC solicitor John Watterson (who also played a crucial part in the issue of the prospectus), outside solicitors Slaughter and May, and no fewer than three independent firms of property valuers.

The first hurdle to be overcome was the different methods of property valuation preferred by NFC and the City institutions respectively. As Mr Butterfield put it:

> We carried out our valuations on a current cost accounting basis (existing use value) and worked out that on that basis our properties were worth around £130 million. I suspect that in the early stages Barclays thought we were a bit of a hick outfit until they realised that we were obeying the recommended rules for Current Cost Accounting, and that they felt our valuations might be unrealistic: that they were in-house valuations to suit our own purposes.

To Mr Tindall, used to seeing properties and their valuations laid out in normal City terms, the initial problem was grasping the unusual property set-up which existed at NFC. The company did not have a full-scale property department that one would normally associate with a public company of similar size and with such an extensive property portfolio, and his initial view was that NFC's property lists 'did not seem to be in very good order'. Moreover, NFC did not seem unduly worried about technicalities of original title on some of their properties: for example the fact that the National Carriers' and

BRS' land came over to them as part of a package deal was good enough for them, since they were using the sites as they had always been used, and had not experienced any problems, but this did not always make them suitable security for an outside third party.

For example, much of the ex-British Rail land still carried complicated rights of way clauses which would reduce, if not entirely eliminate, the value of land for normal commercial use. To bring it back to a domestic analogy, how many people would buy a house if they discovered that someone had the right to drive a railway siding through their back garden?

To give a couple of other examples of the sort of difficulties which arose, NFC's Waste Management subsidiary has a site near Widnes which can be used for the dumping of toxic waste. Such sites are worth money for that purpose, since there are not too many of them about, but from the point of view of bankers' security the professional valuation of the site was nil. On a quite different tack, Fashionflow was part of NFC's National Carriers division, and the legal title to the properties from which they operate was held by National Carriers. The properties themselves, however, appeared in the Fashionflow balance sheet, giving Fashionflow a beneficial interest in the properties. Similar situations existed elsewhere in the group.

The suspicions over different methods of valuation disappeared gradually as the two sides got down to working together. Barclays was reassured by the evidence which Alan Butterfield was able to present which showed that in the year up to the start of the property negotiations NFC had sold exactly 100 properties, of which 99 had fetched the NFC valuation price or even more. Outside professional valuers were called in to look at a sample of other major NFC properties and came up with valuations not far different from those arrived at by NFC's own methods, while Terry Tindall's own investigation of still more properties confirmed this view.

This solved (more or less) the valuation problems since Barclays became much happier about accepting NFC valuations on properties which were not subject to the full rigours of total professional valuation. The bank came to accept that the existing use value adopted by NFC was close enough to the market value figures it was seeking, and it also appreciated that NFC used its own method of valuation as a tool towards deciding which properties it should develop further, and which properties it could sell to advantage.

Another difficulty arose here in that the bank was not dealing with a static list of properties, and NFC's portfolio at the end of the negotiations was markedly different from that at the start of the proceedings. Not only was NFC selling some sites and buying others, it was also retaining properties for new development, sometimes acting the role of developer itself. Even once a provisional list of properties to be charged had been drawn up it was subject to continual revision as some properties were withdrawn, and had to be replaced with others.

The thorny problem of title still had to be resolved, and because of the sheer number of properties involved this could only be done on a sample basis; BMB is reluctant to be drawn too far into detail on this particular point since it has no intention of making a habit of that particular practice and would not like other clients or potential clients to think that it does. But even when title had been established to everyone's satisfaction there was still the laborious task of physically getting hold of the deeds – the actual whereabouts of many was obscure.

Even in the thoroughly comprehensive prospectus property is relegated to a sub-clause in Appendix 11:

In view of the number of properties owned by the NFC Group no examination has been made of title for the purpose of this prospectus. The properties have however, in most cases been owned for many years and the Directors know of no material defects in title.

Terry Tindall was looking for a property mix in several different directions. He wanted a good geographical spread, a good spread between the different operating groups and subsidiaries within NFC and a good spread of properties both in terms of type and size. Thus the properties were spread from the Isle of Wight to Carlisle, and the mortgage value attributed to them went from over £3 million in one instance to as low as £10,000 in another.

The initial 'final list' of property which the clearing bank syndicate agreed to accept as security has a somewhat strange look to it. Apart from anything else, using three independent firms of valuers means that you are getting three separate bases of valuations on different properties: no-one has ever come up with an absolute definition of value and except where an almost perfect market exists – for example in certain parts of the City of London where the rent per square foot is fixed in a competitive market place and the buildings are much of a muchness – different valuers will come up with different figures. It is by no means a precise science, and Barclays was faced with the problem of trying to make the figures from its independent advisers as comparable as possible.

The list falls into three sections. The first, accounting for £21.7 million of the required security, covers 20 of the biggest properties which had been professionally valued, and where there had been a full investigation of title. On this list the mortgage value ascribed to the properties was sometimes higher than NFC's existing use valuation and sometimes lower, while in half a dozen cases the mortgage valuation was taken arbitrarily as just 50 per cent of the NFC existing use valuation.

The second list of 30 properties also amounted to just over £21 million, and here the properties in question had been fully investigated as to the title, but had not undergone full professional valuation: here BMB was sufficiently confident of NFC's own valuation figures, having discovered that both types of valuation were reaching roughly the same conclusion even if by different methods.

Thus well over half of the banks' security lay in just 50

properties, and the remainder was spread over some 200, typically, much smaller, properties, the vast bulk of which were freehold, although there had not been a full investigation of title.

In terms of the breakdown of charged properties as far as NFC was concerned National Carriers bore the biggest brunt, giving £9.5 million of the required security, followed by Pickfords Removals which provided £7 million (with another £1.265 million coming from Pickfords Industrial). Apparently the distribution of charged properties occasionally became a charged issue within NFC itself: when one or more properties was dropped from the schedule for one reason or another, BMB obviously looked for the most convenient replacement, and on at least one occasion a batch of properties from one subsidiary was best fitted to fill the bill. This, according to Terry Tindall, caused some dark murmurings about some people being expected to provide more than their fair share.

There is no doubt that the spirit of co-operation that was engendered during this technical and wearisome sorting out of the property situation was invaluable. Every time the schedule was changed, which was frequently, new valuation and title documents had to be drawn up and sent to all parties for their approval.

Just as it looked as though the property question had been brought finally to a satisfactory solution an unexpected problem cropped up which could have radically altered the whole picture. The 1968 Transport Act which transferred the Sundries Division of British Rail to NFC did not pin down accurately the transfer of properties, and this led to the anomalous situation where the British Railways Board (BRB) had claims on certain National Carriers properties which had been widely regarded as being within the NFC property portfolio. The most difficult part of this to sort out was a warehousing agreement between the two sides which effectively restricted NFC's freedom of action in the use or sale of the properties concerned. Fortunately this last-minute hitch was overcome – partly at least by a trading of properties between NFC and BRB – but it is just one example of the nail-biting times that cropped up all the way through the property negotiations.

10

A MOST UNUSUAL
PROSPECTUS

I seem to remember that in the first 10 or so drafting
meetings we never managed to get beyond page six of the
Prospectus – and that only took us as far as the second page of
Peter Thompson's introductory letter to NFC employees!

> Quote from Michael Hamer, the Barclays
> Merchant Bank director most intimately
> involved in the preparation of the Prospectus.

Ultimately, the reason that a prospectus is such an important
document is because it is asking people to part with money
based on the facts and figures contained therein.

There is no such thing in this world as an easy prospectus.
Every single detail has to be verified, checked, cleared by
solicitors and, in the case of figures, by auditors. All that is
contained within the document has to conform to the Companies Acts' regulations and Stock Exchange requirements –
which means not only that everything included must be
accurate, but also that nothing is missed out that is required by
law or regulations; nor is there any room for ambiguity in the
way that statements are phrased. The directors of the company
have to:

take all reasonable care to ensure that the facts stated herein are true and accurate in all material respects and that there are no other material facts the omission of which would make misleading any statement herein whether of fact or opinion.

Having done that they accept the responsibility for the contents of the prospectus.

All these considerations apply to small straightforward companies with a proven track record which are offering their shares to the public – usually by means of an Offer for Sale through the stock market, so it is not hard to imagine that in the case of NFC p.l.c. the task of preparing a prospectus was one of considerable magnitude. Perhaps the most difficult thing to appreciate is just how many and how varied were the problems facing the principal parties and their advisers. Work had begun on the Prospectus as early as June 24 1981, and at that stage everyone was confident that not just the Prospectus but the whole deal would be completed before the year was out. The document itself was not even completed until the beginning of January 1982, and right up to the last moment final changes were having to be incorporated. Even supposedly normal technical details such as printing and distribution produced considerable headaches. Because of all the unusual and extra data required of the NFC Prospectus it was unusually long – running to 55 pages of which 33 were appendices printed in tiny type, and the print run was a massive 60,000. In addition NFC required illustrations in the form of pictures and diagrams and two-colour printing on a majority of the 55 pages. All the drafts and the three final proofs had to be produced surrounded by secrecy because much of the information contained in them was of a highly sensitive nature. The printers, Williams Lea, must have wondered just what they had let themselves in for as the long and weary process of producing a Prospectus to satisfy everybody dragged on month after month.

Even before the buy-out proposals took shape, accountants throughout NFC had been putting together historical figures and forecasts to prepare the ground for the expected flotation. The new need to produce a Consortium Prospectus to a tight timetable meant a redoubling of efforts to produce information covering the previous five years, audited accounts for the half-year to June 1981 and forecasts for the remainder of the financial year to October 1981. At the same time the accountants were having to play a role in preparing the financial forecasts for the next three years which were the basis for the syndicate banks' involvement. Although these tasks involved all levels of financial management from James Watson down to the chief accountant of the smallest subsidiary, much of the organisation – and indeed much of the work – fell on corporate finance men Tony Morrish and Richard Gerlach. They had to deal with five years' historical information and the forecasts of 50 subsidiary companies, working in conjunction with the Reporting Accountants. For more than two years the Group's accountants were involved almost constantly with auditors, reporting accountants and merchant banks. It was with a great sense of relief that the last few figures were finally slotted into the Prospectus.

Before looking at the Prospectus itself, and at some of the more important problems that cropped up during its preparation, it is worth trying to capture the cauldron-like atmosphere that sometimes existed in the drafting meetings during this long period. It never quite got to the stage of fists actually flying, but tempers ran high on occasions, and the idea of a group of men sitting round a table coolly dissecting problems and producing neat solutions would not stand up to scrutiny for two minutes.

Nobody ever bothered to keep count of the number of meetings that were held during that near-seven month period, but it must have run into hundreds. At the major drafting meetings – with Michael Hamer normally leading for BMB and Philip Mayo for NFC, supported by company secretary Jim Staley – there were hardly ever less than a dozen people in attendance, and it was not uncommon for there to be twice that number there. All of them wanted to achieve a common end, but different groups had different positions to defend and in many cases compromise was not easy to reach. It was not unusual for meetings to start after normal working hours – often at the offices of Barclays Merchant Bank in Gracechurch Street in the City of London and when, as happened not infrequently, five or six hours negotiation between men who had already put in a full day's work left them apparently no further forward on a particularly sticky point, it is little wonder that frustration and aggravation crept in. Even when the negotiators reached home they did not always get away from the document, as bulkily-clad, black-helmeted motorcycle messengers brought Prospectus proofs hot from the City printers at all hours, livening up the tranquil neighbourhoods where senior executives tend to live.

A prospectus can be roughly divided into two parts: statutory information that the company is required to give, and other information that the company itself wants to give in order to describe itself more fully than the basic disclosure of activities demanded by law, and any other non-statutory disclosure which it thinks will improve the attractiveness of the proposition which it is putting forward. The crucial point here is that the non-statutory information offered must be guaranteed as being as accurate in every respect as the mandatory disclosures.

It is perhaps in this area that the Consortium's biggest single difficulty lay, and it was probably the main reason why the drafting took so long to get past page six. The Consortium was not making an open offer for sale to a sophisticated and virtually limitless investment public. It was pitching its offer on a highly restricted basis inviting a clearly defined and relatively narrow group of people to subscribe for shares, and most of these people had never before even considered the possibility of direct share ownership.

In Philip Mayo's words:

Our Prospectus had to teach as well as inform. We could not

assume that our prospective investors knew anything about the way a company is organised and run. We needed to be able to make very simple statements like 'dividends are paid from profits; so, no profits, no dividends' without having them caveated out of all recognition.

As Michael Hamer of BMB put it delicately in retrospect:

We had an unusual problem in that our client was not oversympathetic to the idea of having to produce the normal Companies Act prospectus.

Roughly translated, that means that there was a not a little aggravation from time to time between the bank and its client. What was at issue of course was to make the prospectus as intelligible and optimistic – and as comprehensible – as possible for an unsophisticated audience while at the same time making sure that every detail was still correct in law, and in a sense Barclays was wearing two hats at the meetings since it was financial adviser to the Consortium, but also had to represent the interests of the syndicate of banks which it was putting together to undertake the loan finance without which the deal would founder altogether. And although it was the Consortium's Prospectus, BMB was making the offer for subscription on its behalf.

A certain piquancy was added to the situation, because the medium-term loan and the loan for working capital were anyway conditional on a minimum level of subscription for shares from NFC employees and pensioners. Had that minimum not been achieved there would have been no bank loans and the National Freight Consortium p.l.c. would not now own National Freight Company, but would merely have become one of the thousands of other companies lodged with the Registrar of Companies which were not trading.

Just to keep the pot bubbling nicely there were three firms of solicitors involved: Ashurst Morris Crisp were solicitors to the

Consortium and the Offer, Freshfields looked after the interests of NFC group, and Slaughter and May were solicitors to BMB in its role as agent for the banks. Also on hand were Duncan C. Fraser & Co., consulting actuaries to the Pension Trustee, and of course Ernst & Whinney, the auditors and reporting accountants. Each of these had positive stances to defend and it would have been a real miracle if disagreements and some very hard bargaining had not taken place.

These drafting meetings were by no means the whole story. The directors who would have to stand behind the Prospectus were looking at the implications of what was to be published in their name. In both Bedford and London, meetings sometimes ran late into the night. None had a greater impact on the directors as individuals than the meeting at the City Road offices towards the end of 1981 when each of the directors was asked to commit himself irrevocably to the money he was prepared to invest. At the end of a long evening session, Peter Thompson told his colleagues what he was putting in, and asked them to state their firm commitments. These figures, published in the Prospectus, show that the total amount was well in excess of BMB's stipulated minimum.

Few people read even simple prospectuses from cover to cover and that includes institutions whose job it is to invest other people's money and charge them for so doing. (Even although it occurred some years ago, the mention of the collapse of Mersey Docks and Harbour Board will still produce red faces in some City boardrooms, because many institutions were happily under the misapprehension that the Board's loans carried a government guarantee. Subsequent scrutiny of the small print proved – too late – that this was not the case.)

By no stretch of the imagination could the NFC Prospectus be regarded as simple, and it was obvious that Peter Thompson had to make as big an impact on potential investors as early as possible before they got bogged down in a welter of technical and financial data: pro-forma profit and loss accounts and balance sheets are not everyone's cup of tea. In spite of the tremendous communications exercise which had taken place to educate and inform the workforce about the Consortium's concept, progress and plans (of which more later), it was on the Prospectus and accompanying share application forms that the success or failure of the whole venture would rest.

It is a compliment to those involved in drafting the final product that Mr Thompson's letter to his colleagues reads as well as it does, considering the number of times it was unravelled and knitted back together again. But indications of meticulous drafting are still in evidence: for example, 'on behalf of its (the Consortium's) Directors I am inviting you to buy shares', – not 'I think you should buy shares'. And under the heading 'why invest?' Mr Thompson states carefully: 'I believe there are four good reasons why this is a good time to invest in this enterprise', – not 'I think you should invest in this enterprise'. Undoubtedly Peter Thompson would have liked to have gone a good deal further in spelling out his optimism – and so far at least events would have proved him right. But he could not completely avoid the restraining hands of financial advisers and lawyers.

At the same time Mr Thompson had to reinforce the idea of NFC as one group rather than a conglomerate of largely independent subsidiaries. For the Consortium idea to work, all 25,000 NFC employees had to start regarding themselves as members of the same family. Again this message had been rammed home in the intensive communications campaign, but even so it was felt it had to be reinforced in the Prospectus itself. Obviously the wording of what he said about the various divisions and subsidiaries had to be carefully vetted, but there is another aspect here which offers a splendid example of the minute attention to detail involved in producing a prospectus.

Brian Cottee, as head of communications at NFC, was obviously much involved in the presentation of the end product: prospectuses with no illustrations do not exactly leap out at the eye. He therefore prepared two pages of montage photographs which had the dual purpose of helping to break up the solid text, and also to give a visual indication of NFC's activities. He also insisted on the use of a readable size of type where possible and the use of a little colour in headings, panels etc to brighten the document. Each page of pictures carried the heading 'Some Examples of Products of the NFC Group', but this was queried by the lawyers on the grounds that some of the activities shown should more properly be termed as services; with these sort of discussions it is easy to see how tempers can fray and seven months slip by.

Even once all these problems had been resolved the NFC Prospectus was a most unusual animal. When it gets down to statutory information there is little scope for straying from the standard format, but even here the Consortium managed to cajole some simplification in wording from the lawyers and accountants. But the major problems lay in the unique nature of the proposals being put forward, in the number of supplementary schemes required to make the whole project feasible, and on the fact that many of these schemes, which would have to be incorporated in the Prospectus, were still being worked on as the prospectus was in the process of preparation.

Most businesses seeking outside capital for the first time have a proven track record, an established capital structure and have been run by roughly the same book of rules – the Articles of Association which form the bible of what a company can and cannot do – for a number of years at least. Not one of these applied to the Consortium. When the Prospectus was being drawn up the Consortium was just a group of people with an organising committee of 14 (three of whom formed the initial Board) trying to raise money to buy an existing business from the Government. True, that business had a track record, but under the Consortium solution it would have a completely different capital structure – which meant that all the previous figures had to be re-calculated to show what they would be like had the proposed new structure been in operation in the past. And although all the members of the Consortium had been

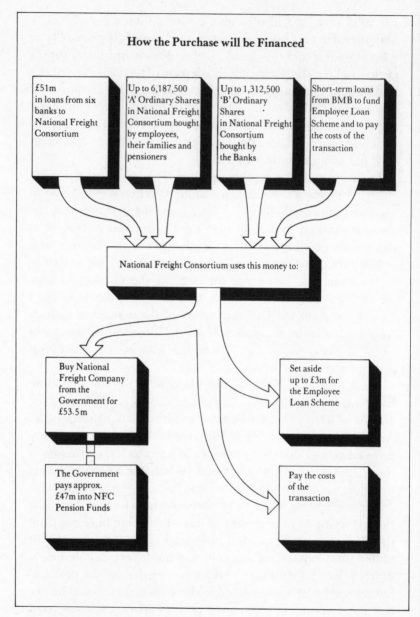

How the Purchase will be Financed

£51m
in loans from six
banks to
National Freight
Consortium

Up to 6,187,500
'A' Ordinary Shares
in National Freight
Consortium bought
by employees,
their families and
pensioners

Up to 1,312,500
'B' Ordinary
Shares
in National Freight
Consortium
bought by
the Banks

Short-term loans
from BMB to fund
Employee Loan
Scheme and to pay
the costs of the
transaction

National Freight Consortium uses this money to:

Buy National
Freight Company
from the
Government for
£53.5m

Set aside
up to £3m for
the Employee
Loan Scheme

The Government
pays approx.
£47m into NFC
Pension Funds

Pay the costs
of the
transaction

The NFC Prospectus was unusual, as these example pages show.

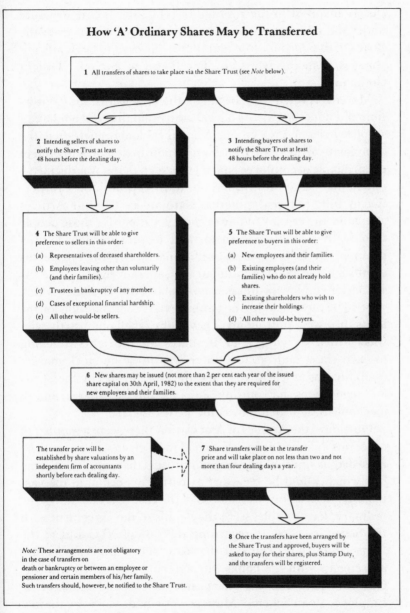

How 'A' Ordinary Shares May be Transferred

1 All transfers of shares to take place via the Share Trust (see *Note* below).

2 Intending sellers of shares to notify the Share Trust at least 48 hours before the dealing day.

3 Intending buyers of shares to notify the Share Trust at least 48 hours before the dealing day.

4 The Share Trust will be able to give preference to sellers in this order:

(a) Representatives of deceased shareholders.

(b) Employees leaving other than voluntarily (and their families).

(c) Trustees in bankruptcy of any member.

(d) Cases of exceptional financial hardship.

(e) All other would-be sellers.

5 The Share Trust will be able to give preference to buyers in this order:

(a) New employees and their families.

(b) Existing employees (and their families) who do not already hold shares.

(c) Existing shareholders who wish to increase their holdings.

(d) All other would-be buyers.

6 New shares may be issued (not more than 2 per cent each year of the issued share capital on 30th April, 1982) to the extent that they are required for new employees and their families.

The transfer price will be established by share valuations by an independent firm of accountants shortly before each dealing day.

7 Share transfers will be at the transfer price and will take place on not less than two and not more than four dealing days a year.

Note: These arrangements are not obligatory in the case of transfers on death or bankruptcy or between an employee or pensioner and certain members of his/her family. Such transfers should, however, be notified to the Share Trust.

8 Once the transfers have been arranged by the Share Trust and approved, buyers will be asked to pay for their shares, plus Stamp Duty, and the transfers will be registered.

The diagrams on these two pages explain simply how the buy-out would be financed and how the internal share-transfer scheme would work.

closely involved in the running of NFC, the Board structure under the new system was to be markedly different from the Board of the Corporation, and there were even to be significant changes from the relatively new Board of National Freight Company.

Moreover, when work began on the Prospectus, the Consortium did not even exist as a legal entity and thus did not have a set of Articles of Association. When these had been drafted, the complexity of the share transfer mechanism designed to protect the principle of employee control was such that it was decided – reluctantly – that these provisions must appear in the Prospectus in full. (Normal practice is to make the full Articles available for scrutiny at one or more locations for those people who really want to see them, and to provide only a brief summary in the prospectus itself.) Specifically, the Prospectus would have to include in detail the separate rights of the 'A' shares for employees and pensioners, and the 'B' shares which were to be those held by the banks as part consideration for the loans they were putting up. They had to spell out exactly who was entitled to own 'A' and 'B' shares and the rights attaching to each class, and because there was to be no stock market quotation for at least five years, they had to specify the terms and conditions for putting a value on the shares and a mechanism by which they could be transferred.

Outside of the Articles of Association there were a number of other bits of information which had to be given which would be regarded as unusual in a normal prospectus – and even some bits which would be regarded as perfectly normal in the vast majority of cases but were not so in the case of NFC. Out of the ordinary, for example, were the details of the agreement with the Secretary of State regarding the sale of NFC Ltd to the Consortium, full details of the loan, subscription and other agreements with the banks, the agreements reached with the Government for funding the pension deficits, and details of the Employee Loan Scheme. Matters were made worse by the fact that in the case of most of these, the people employed in drawing up the Prospectus were operating on continually shifting sand. The Employee Loan Scheme, the Employee Share Trust, the pension negotiations and the bank loan agreements were all being negotiated and altered as the Prospectus was being prepared, and the document had to be amended accordingly in each case.

Indeed, finalising the loan agreements was a major task because during the period of negotiation with the banks, from the initial presentation in April through the frenzied calculations during May and June to the agreement of the offer by the syndicate of banks in October, a lot of attention had been paid to the general conditions of loan finance but no detailed work had been done on the form of the loan agreements. The main terms of the loans had been discussed with BMB and set out in an appendix to the information document presented to the syndicate banks in October. However, the detailed drafting had to await approval of the 1981 Companies Act and this was finally given in November. Barclays, through Alan Brown, instructed Slaughter and May to draw up agreements as solicitors for the syndicate banks – it seemed almost to be an afterthought, a technical detail to be completed. But the drafting took much longer than anticipated and when the first draft finally appeared the size of the task became apparent. This first draft ran to some 150 pages and covered both the medium term loan and the trading finance agreement. Putting into legal jargon a loan involving 19 guarantors and six lending banks with title secured on some 270 properties was, to say the least, complex.

A gruelling round of negotiations followed. The meetings were at the offices of Slaughter and May and involved James Watson and NFC Treasurer Hugh Mellor backed up by Freshfields, acting as solicitors for the guarantors. BMB were present, but this time acting as agents for the lending banks and not in their customary role as advisers to the Consortium. Inevitably this posed problems: at the first meeting a substantial number of changes had to be made before the Consortium was happy that the arrangements would be workable in practice. Only after the third draft were the points of difference narrowed down to a few very specific and detailed items which were cleared after reference back to the Consortium Board and the lending banks.

The Consortium representatives at these meetings had then just enough time to adjust their concentration to deal with the task of arranging that each of the guarantors would comply in full with the 1981 Companies Act requirements. This was thought to be the first practical application of the 1981 Act in which the old restrictions preventing companies from supporting the financing of their own shares had been partly demolished. The new restrictions, although more liberal, were nonetheless complex, requiring reports from 20 teams of auditors and meetings involving every director of every guarantor company to certify their individual and collective support for the loan agreements and the various mortgages and guarantees supporting them.

An unexpected difficulty arose in preparing a list of the active subsidiary and associated companies of the NFC Group. Normally this exercise is a virtual formality, but because of NFC's previous structure considerable discussion was required to decide what constituted subsidiaries and what constituted associate companies, and it was virtually at the last minute that these difficulties were resolved. But a much graver last-minute problem hove into view, and this was the considerable downgrading of profit forecasts filtering through from the NFC divisions which resulted from them preparing their 1982 budgets and forecasts on a more conservative basis. After prolonged heartsearching it was decided that these new forecasts would have to be incorporated in the, by now well advanced, Prospectus, and a whole week from December 11 to December 18 was taken up in recalculating the figures in line with the new, lower forecasts.

When it was published in the middle of January, the Prospectus won considerable acclaim in the financial Press as one of the most informative, comprehensive and readable documents to shareholders or potential shareholders that the respective City Editors had ever seen. That may provide some slight comfort to those people who spent tens of thousands of man hours in its preparation – and who received that last major piece of the jigsaw puzzle, the agreement on short term finance with the banks, just two days before Christmas – or exactly six months to the day from the first preliminary meeting to discuss the putting together of the Prospectus.

But perhaps their greatest satisfaction will come from the knowledge that at the end of the day the results of that Prospectus were to be a resounding vote of confidence in the Consortium and its plans for a future NFC substantially owned by the people who worked for it.

11

THE FINAL PACKAGE DEAL

Offer for Subscription to employees and their immediate
families and pensioners of National Freight Company
Limited of up to 6,187,500 'A' Ordinary Shares payable in
full on application.

> Introduction to the Prospectus of National
> Freight Consortium p.l.c.

After all these months of conceptual thinking, basic planning,
argument, discussion, and negotiations – ranging from Cabinet
Minister level through some of the top City names and right
down to the shop floor – just what was the deal the Consortium
was offering at the end of the day? Who exactly was eligible to
buy shares and on what terms, and what businesses and
management were they buying for their money? What conditions were attached to share purchase, and perhaps most
important of all, what sort of return could shareholders
reasonably expect on their investment: were they likely to see
capital appreciation on their shares, and what was the likely
income in prospect from dividends paid out on their shares?

In spite of the best efforts of the Consortium and its advisers
to spell out the options as simply as possible, and to give as
much information as possible in readily understandable terms,
these were all questions that potential investors had to ask

themselves, and there were others too: would they have greater job security in a company which they effectively owned, and would a future Labour Government carry out its renationalisation threat, possibly on terms disadvantageous to NFC p.l.c.'s worker shareholders?

First and foremost Peter Thompson and his colleagues were offering the workforce the opportunity not just of worker participation in the ownership of NFC, but of a controlling shareholding in the group which would make employee shareholders collective masters of the company's destiny. In this context they would be in the same position as shareholders in any other public company: they would not, as shareholders anyway, take part in the day to day running of the business, but would have enough votes to support or block any outside takeover bid for the company, vote on any major structural changes – for example big acquisitions or alterations in the capital structure – and would have a say in the appointment or re-election of directors.

As Peter Thompson stated in his letter to shareholders this aspect of the deal was mainly defensive in principle: NFC was going to be privatised anyway, and the only question was how. Would it not be better for that decision to be taken by NFC members rather than the Government or anonymous outside shareholders? But there was also a positive aspect which, it transpired, was important to many people in an emotive way. It allowed a new sense of 'belonging' and a chance to show their faith in themselves and their companies by putting their own savings, or even borrowed money, into the enterprise they worked for.

The Consortium in which entitled people were invited to invest had an original authorised capital of £10 million, of which it was the intention to issue £7.5 million initially. Entitled NFC members, families and pensioners were being invited to subscribe for up to 82.5 per cent of that capital in the form of 'A' shares, while the remaining 17.5 per cent was to be in the form of 'B' shares which were to be issued to the banks who were providing the loan capital to buy the company from the Government, and the £30 million working capital facility required by the Consortium.

There were to be certain differences in voting rights between the 'A' shareholders and the 'B' shareholders. Both classes would rank equally for dividends, and in the unlikely event of the Consortium being wound up, or making a capital distribution, for that too. But, in order to look after the interests of the banks, the 'B' shareholders would have the automatic right to appoint a director to the Consortium Board of Directors as long as the 'B' shareholders retained 5 per cent or more of the issued capital, and that director would not be subject to re-election on a rotation basis in the same way as the other Consortium Board directors. Another privilege of the minority 'B' shareholders was the right of veto on the increase in the number of 'A' shares that were in issue, above a small agreed amount each year to be set aside to allow new NFC employees to take advantage of the right to become shareholders. This clause was inserted to prevent the proportion of 'B' shares falling too rapidly in relation to the number of 'A' shares in issue.

The proposed 82.5 per cent/17.5 per cent split was not originally fixed rigidly, rather it represented the maximum proportion of shares to be held by eligible NFC members and the minimum that would be allocated to the banks. However, for the Consortium proposals to succeed the NFC side would have to subscribe a minimum of £4.125 million under agreements with the banks, and of that at least £2.125 million would have to come from sources other than the special Employee Loan Scheme which the Consortium had set up to help people buy shares. In other words, there had to be a minimum financial commitment on the part of NFC employees and other eligible purchasers to confirm that this was to be a genuine staff buy-out, but the banks, on top of their 875,000 'B' shares, would probably have found a means of underwriting any small shortfall in subscriptions for 'A' shares rather than see the deal fall through.

Eligibility was another thorny problem to be settled before the Prospectus was finalised. For political considerations (including the hovering spectre of renationalisation under a Labour Government) and commercial reasons (to create as wide a market as possible in shares that were not to be traded on the stock market for at least five years) it was desirable that the offer to subscribe should be open to as many people as possible. On the other hand they should not be so widely spread that the vision of the genuine staff buy-out was lost and also eligibility had to be clearly defined.

Technical rules and regulations prevented NFC employees outside of the United Kingdom and the Channel Islands from applying, but that apart the net for those eligible for shares was cast as widely as possible. All permanent employees of NFC from directors down to probationary staff could apply for shares, and this right also extended to immediate families. These were defined as wives or husbands, children including step-children and adopted children, and grandchildren, including again step- and adopted grandchildren.

Pensioners were included on both moral and practical grounds – as explained in the Pensions chapter, which also outlined the adopted doctrine of making eligible those in receipt of pensions. But those eligible also included husbands and wives of pensioners together with widows and widowers.

This pretty well covered the field of those eligible, and produced a total figure of some 40,000 people and their families. But inevitably there were certain anomalies – few in number and relatively unimportant to the eventual outcome, but interesting as yet another example of the intricacies involved.

One thing which changed between early drafts of the proposed Consortium solution and the final Prospectus was that no-one was obliged to buy shares. The early drafts before even the go-ahead in principle from Mr Fowler had incorporated the idea that new managers would be expected to buy shares, but this idea had been dropped before the 'Concordat' between the Consortium and the Secretary of State had been agreed. Instead, the share structure of the company allowed the issue of an extra 2 per cent of 'A' shares each year to guarantee new members the option to join other employee shareholders. By the same token no-one could be forced to *sell* shares even if they left NFC.

There were other unusual rules governing the 'A' shares laid down in the Prospectus. In order to encourage as wide a share ownership as possible, no-one, including family holdings, was to be entitled to more than 100,000 shares in total, and although the Articles of Association allowed the normal one vote per share, this was restricted to shareholdings which did not exceed 20 per cent held either by an individual or a group of individuals acting in concert, unless this holding resulted from a bona fide offer within the rules of the City Code on Takeovers or mergers. When this was not the case, the Articles allowed the voting power of such very large proportional holdings to be restricted.

These provisions dealt with the big boys, but because the Consortium wanted as wide a spread of shareholding as possible it also took action to help people to buy shares even if they did not have the ready cash available. An Employee Loan Scheme was set up to be administered by the Consortium under the terms of the 1948 Companies' Act whereby Barclays made up to £3 million available to the Consortium, and the Consortium was able to use this money to make interest-free loans of up to £200 to NFC members for the purchase of 'A' shares, repayments to be made over a one year period by equal instalments deducted from wages or salaries.

For the NFC loan scheme only employees were eligible, and if applications under this scheme exceeded the £3 million available, then all applications would be reduced pro rata. In the end that clause did not have to be invoked.

One of the most important questions for potential shareholders was the marketability and valuation of their shares.

Since there was to be no stock market quotation there would be no free market where the shares could change hands on any working day, and the absence of normal market forces meant that the price of the shares would not necessarily find its own level at which the demands of willing buyers and willing sellers was equally matched. What NFC shareholders were offered as an alternative was an independent Share Trust which would handle the transfer of shares between buyers and sellers, and an independent valuation of the shares not less than twice a year and not more than four times a year. Except in cases of death or bankruptcy, or transfer of shares within a family unit, shares could not be transferred direct between shareholders and could only be dealt in four times a year on appointed 'Dealing Days'. Dealings would only be possible to the extent that the Share Trust was able to match willing buyers and sellers at the 'Transfer Price' (i.e. the independent valuation put on the shares by a chosen firm of accountants). The only flexibility in these arrangements, and it was very little, was that each year the Trustees would have a small number of extra shares available to allocate to new employees, and the Trust was to be allowed to hold a small 'float of shares' so that it could iron out any small imbalance that might exist between buyers and sellers on Dealing Day. Normally, the transfer price would be published a reasonable time before the next dealing day, and all buyers and sellers wishing to deal at that price would have to give the Share Trust at least 48 hours notice of their dealing requirements.

One problem here was that willing buyers and sellers were most unlikely to match at the given transfer price at any one time, and therefore the trustees would have to list categories in order of priority for both buyers and sellers. Since the Trust and not the Consortium would be responsible for choosing the order of priority, the Prospectus could not give a definitive order of preference, but it did give an example of a likely outcome. For buyers the list was:

   i.   new employees and their families
   ii.   existing employees and families not already holding shares
   iii.   existing shareholders wishing to increase their stake
   iv.   other would-be eligible buyers

For sellers the order of precedence was:

   i.   representatives of deceased shareholders
   ii.   employees leaving the group on a non-voluntary basis
   iii.   cases of bankruptcy
   iv.   cases of extreme financial hardship
   v.   other would-be sellers

The fact remained however that if there was a big imbalance between potential buyers and potential sellers a gap would exist which the trustees could not bridge. In good times when demand for shares was high, many potential buyers would not be able to get the shares they wanted, and if the company should fall on hard times many people wishing to sell might not be able to find a matching buyer, and so would be locked in to their shareholding even if they no longer considered it a good investment.

That covers the more technical aspects of the package that would-be shareholders had to take into their considerations, but what about the all-important trading and financial outlook for the Consortium? After all it had been NFC's patchy profit record that had put a normal Offer for Sale out of the reckoning.

When shareholders are considering an investment in a company they are usually concerned most with current and future profits, current and future dividends, and the likely effect of these on the value of their shares. They may also take note of the asset backing to their shares, since this can become an important factor in valuing those shares if the company decides to sell off major divisions, or if it is on the receiving end of a takeover bid. Historical information can be useful – for example some companies or industries have an established cyclical pattern of trading, but such historical information may be of little relevance if the company concerned is going through a period of major management re-organisation, or is making a considerable change in its pattern of trading. Also different companies adopt different policies in relation to dividend payments: some adjust their dividends upwards or downwards in line with each year's trading performance, while others prefer to maintain a steady dividend policy of either maintaining or slightly increasing their dividend each year irrespective of the year's trading (barring of course total disaster). In those companies there will be years when the dividend is covered several times over by the earnings attributable to holders of the Ordinary shares, while in other years the Board may recommend payments which are actually more than the amount earned, making up the balance from reserves built up in previous good years.

Potential NFC investors had some of these factors to go on, but not all. The Consortium, being new, had no back record of dividend payments, but indicated that on predicted profits for the financial year ending October 2 it would pay a dividend equivalent of 10.7p per share before basic rate income tax. Had it been a full financial year October to October the recommended dividend would have been the equivalent of 14.3p per share.

Since the shares were being offered at par this meant that on the prospectus forecast shareholders were being offered a fairly handsome gross yield of 14.3 per cent on their initial investment of 100p per share. This was roughly in line with the NFC policy of paying dividends at least sufficient to cover the cost of the interest paid by shareholders who had borrowed money to buy shares (apart, of course, from the £200 interest-free loan entitlement). But the proposed initial dividends meant rather more than that: although no longer-term forecasts were offered in the Prospectus, the financial advisers involved would not have put their names behind a dividend level that they did not believe could be at least maintained in the future.

The forecast dividend was based on a pre-tax profit estimate of £4.3 million in the period to October 3 1981, the last three months of which consisted of unaudited figures taken from management accounts. NFC's previous profit record over the past five years had been nothing to write home about in terms of consistency, but at least the £4.3 million figure from October 1980 to October 1981 represented a recovery from the disastrous slump in 1980 profits caused by the depression and the loss of the BREPS contract. However, anyone with an analytical turn of mind would immediately notice two factors giving cause for possible concern. The first was that NFC's pre-tax profit figures were consistently struck after taking into account profit on disposal of property, and secondly, the forecast 1981 profits would turn out quite differently when calculated under the new Consortium capital structure: pension liabilities allowed for would disappear, but would be replaced by a considerably larger sum payable to the banks as interest on loans to the Consortium. The net effect of these changes would be to reduce the forecast pre-tax profit to £1.2 million.

Coming back to property, most public companies treat profits on property sales as one-off, non-recurring items, and so do not include them in the profit and loss account. Had NFC chosen to follow that practice the forecasts for the year to the beginning of October 1981 would have been for a net loss before tax, although still a considerably smaller loss than would have appeared in the 1980 calendar year figures calculated on the same basis. NFC had two answers to criticism along these lines. The first was that property profits had been a regular item for some years, and would continue to be so in the near future, so that it was legitimate to treat them as genuine profits rather than exceptional items. Secondly, by selling these properties the group was not consuming its own seed corn: in the five years to December 1980 NFC group had realised £27 million from the sale of properties, but over the same period had actually made new property investment of £28 million.

On paper, the most comfortable aspect of the proposed share

issue was the asset backing for the shares offered for subscription. With the offer fully subscribed each 100p share was backed by assets of 516p. This sounds like a comfortable cushion, but the figure really only means anything if the company is to be taken over, wound up or if it is to undertake a capital reduction. Since the whole point of the Consortium solution was to prevent any of these eventualities they could safely be discarded, and in the meantime assets, whatever their balance sheet value, are only worth what they produce.

Ultimately therefore, the investment decision lay with signs of recovery and reconstruction, optimism expressed by management and reflected in the generous dividend forecast, and people's faith in their own business. The confidence shown by the banks in their willingness to lend large sums of money was another plus point, but probably the decisive factor was the ability of the Consortium to communicate with, and harness the enthusiasm of, more than a quarter of its employees eligible to buy shares.

12

THE CRUCIAL ROLE OF
COMMUNICATIONS

We are the largest concern in Britain ever to have attempted
to take control over our own destiny . . . this idea didn't come
from the Government. It was *our* idea.

> Peter Thompson, quoted from the NFC
> booklet 'Buying our own Company'.

The Cabal had accepted early on that motivating enough
people to apply for shares was the really crucial factor in the
whole exercise.

> Extract from a paper on buy-out
> communications prepared by Brian Cottee.

It was perfectly obvious from the genesis of the consortium
solution that one of the prerequisites for success would be a
massive campaign of educating, informing and persuading
people that this novel idea was in their best interests. Clearly,
financial benefits in the technical form of future dividends and
possible capital appreciation would not be enough to ensure
success, and some 40,000 NFC employees and pensioners – or
at least a good proportion of them – had to be convinced that

this was their scheme, and that NFC p.l.c. would be their company: a simple management buy-out would never have been able to raise the necessary funds, and nor would it have fulfilled the Consortium's genuine visionary aim of constructing an entirely new type of industrial structure. It was equally obvious that this massive communications exercise would have to be tackled at crash speed, since the original timetable aimed at publishing the Prospectus in September, and having the whole deal sewn up by October.

Although the main thrust of the communications exercise had to be aimed at those eligible to buy shares, other areas could not be overlooked: good national and trade Press coverage had to be sought, MPs on both sides of the House had to be kept informed, and discussions held with trades unions to encourage them at least towards a neutral stance if not positively a favourable one. As has been seen from earlier chapters, the Consortium had to sell its idea to the City to get the idea off the ground in the first place and the communications aspect of the Prospectus rated high on the list of priorities. However this chapter is primarily concerned with employee and pensioner communications, and to a lesser extent with Press relations.

The hub of the NFC communications network in the Bedford headquarters is usually an area of frenetic activity. From here four people (including a secretary) operate the NFC's corporate communications, producing many of the internal publications and information bulletins, fielding Press calls, and other demands for information from outside. It is also their job to scan press cuttings and draw the attention of head office managers or subsidiary companies to items of interest or concern to them. Added to this they are largely responsible for arranging conferences and providing any visual aids. In their spare time the communications department have lunch, and every time I walk into Brian Cottee's domain, I am irresistibly reminded of walking into the news room of a newspaper. Although not on the Board, Mr Cottee attends Executive

Board meetings and most major strategy meetings to add his views on communications aspects of plans and programmes being drawn up by the Board. This close link between top management and the people directly responsible for communication with employees is still an unbridged gap in much of British industry.

When it became clear in April 1981 that the Offer for Sale route was likely to be abandoned in favour of the consortium solution there had to be a swift re-think on strategy, and the Offer for Sale programme was shelved. However, groundwork already done towards that end was to prove distinctly useful: NFC had taken an outside financial public relations consultants, Universal McCann, to help pave the way for a stock market quotation by making sure that the powerful financial Press was fully informed about the – until then – largely anonymous NFC. In 1980 McCann's had arranged a series of informal lunches with City Editors and senior financial journalists, and this stood NFC in good stead when the buy-out idea was announced, since it received almost unanimously favourable Press comment. In the normal course of events, favourable financial coverage in the national Press filters through to the trade Press who tend to be less financially clued up than the specialists (in the same way that the financial specialists cull the trade Press to fill in the gaps in their information on technical and detailed matters). NFC already had good relations with the freight press, and so had the valuable backing of independent Press comment in both the national and trade Press (plus radio and TV coverage) to back its own internal thrust.

That can be regarded as something of a bonus, but there is still no doubt at all that the fate of the Consortium rested fairly and squarely in its own hands: at the end of the day it was only by inspiring senior and middle management, to the extent that they could communicate their enthusiasm right down the line to drivers and warehousemen, that the Consortium and the Organising Committee could hope to generate the level of

The buy-out received extensive and sustained Press interest and support.
These were typical national headlines.

support required. Fortunately they had several things going for them right from the start.

If one had to pick the most important single factor it would almost certainly be Peter Thompson himself. His own enthusiasm for the project was unbounded, and this enthusiasm automatically rubbed off on other people. One of the earliest decisions taken when the communications programme was being worked out was to harness this enthusiasm and point it in the right directions where it would do most good. Another priceless advantage was that Mr Thompson was well liked within NFC and two small stories will serve to illustrate that point.

Some months after the buy-out had been completed I asked a young depot manager of one of NFC's subsidiaries why he had been persuaded to buy shares. Part of his reply was, 'there's nothing snooty about this company. If Peter Thompson walked into this (shareholders') meeting now he would recognise me, and know me by name.' The second example is rather more anecdotal: at NFC's first Annual General Meeting there was one wag of a shareholder out of the massive turnout who insisted on voting against the re-election of every director so that, technically, the resolutions could not be passed unanimously. But when it came to votes against Peter Thompson's re-election even this stalwart kept his hand down: technically, Peter Thompson was the only director to be re-elected unanimously.

Peter Thompson's own personality is, of course, reflected in what he likes to call the 'participative management style' which NFC has been pursuing over the last few years. Although there are obvious administrative difficulties in dealing with a 25,000 workforce spread around more than 700 locations, there are also definite advantages in that real responsibility stretches a long way down the line. Also the number of staff at each location is small on average: on a straight arithmetic calculation it works out at around 35. This has made for good informal communication between management and staff at local level, and has been a contributory factor to NFC's excellent industrial relations record.

Against this background the communications package was put together – at this stage with a September Prospectus in mind, and in consultation with McCanns on some aspects. The underlying principle that was adopted was to make sure that employees, and also pensioners wherever possible, should be the first to hear about the scheme and the first to be given news of subsequent developments. They should not, as so often happens, receive official notification after reading about it in the papers. On the other hand, within this constraint, the media should be kept fully informed of developments as comprehensively as possible in order to build on the goodwill already established in that area, but emphasis should be laid on the fact that management and workforce were receiving just as extensive information.

The programme devised by the communications department had three principal aims: to inform, to educate, and to enthuse. Under the information heading there were two main objectives. The second was to get people in the individual divisions and subsidiaries to think NFC – for instance to get across to drivers and warehousemen that they were in a group which also ran a big chain of travel agents, stored chemicals at a tank farm and handled waste disposal. Equally the girl behind the desk at Pickfords Travel selling package tours to Majorca had to be aware that she was part of a group which owned a fleet of more than 16,000 vehicles distributing parcels and freight up and down the country 24 hours a day.

The first, which could not have been achieved without the second, was to let everyone know what the buy-out was all about; to explain the reasons for it, the advantages of it and the structure that would emerge at the end of it. An understanding of the underlying concept was fundamental to the whole project. The educational aspect involved teaching people how public companies worked, how the shareholder principle worked and what it meant to own shares. This sounds relatively straightforward but it was, in fact, a delicate exercise. Many of NFC's managers and most of its workforce had no knowledge at all in this area, and many of them had political or even emotional objections to the idea. It is only share scandals which hit the headlines and although these represent a tiny minority of deals done and a very, very small amount of harm done when measured against the benefits of a free market economy dominated by public limited companies, the disproportionate amount of publicity they receive has led many non-financial people to equate dealing in stocks and shares with Mr Edward Heath's famous 'unacceptable face of capitalism'. This was a ghost which had to be laid.

The enthusiasm aspect rested, as has already been indicated, largely in the hands of Peter Thompson. He was the leader and prime mover of the Consortium and it was he who, either directly or indirectly, had to carry the workforce with him.

This was one of the reasons which prompted Brian Cottee to press for a videotape presentation as the main thrust of direct employee presentations, on the grounds that written messages and word of mouth contact, however punchily presented, would not have sufficient force – or consistency. And Peter Thompson certainly could not undertake a 700-plus whistle-stop tour round the country on top of all his other commitments. But whatever the merits of the suggestion, the swift acceptance of it was a brave move on the part of the Consortium: preparation of video presentations is a highly specialised field, NFC had very little expertise in the technique, and time was running short.

The Consortium therefore brought in another firm of specialists, Wadlow Grosvenor Productions, who would actually produce the video programme based on a draft requirement and outline script drawn up by NFC Communications Department with an input from McCanns. In the meantime the department was working out a timetable for the presentations to be made and taking steps to hire the substantial amount of technical equipment that would be needed to make the required number of presentations in the extremely short time available. Brian Cottee and his staff calculated they would need 65 video players and about the same number of TV monitors to get through all the presentations in the two weeks allotted, but discovered to their chagrin that NFC did not have a monopoly on the demand for rented video equipment at that time: there was a small matter of a Royal Wedding coming up which everybody and his brother (or more possibly mother) wanted to record for posterity. What should have been a formality of hiring video equipment in bulk turned out to be more difficult than anticipated, and although the problem was overcome it adds a new dimension to NFC's timing problems: to have privatisation delayed initially by extraneous business factors, and the Consortium prospectus subsequently delayed by legal problems, can be regarded as normal commercial hazards, but to have a crash communications exercise almost thwarted because it clashed with The Wedding of the century is not the sort of contingency normally allowed for in forward business planning.

However, Granada TV Rental (based like NFC in Bedford) finally obliged, and arranged for the sets and back-up equipment to be available at 60 key spots round the country, with technicians alerted in case of hitches, and while the video itself was being prepared the communications department of NFC was writing scripts and researching background notes for the managers who would do the presentations on location.

By this time the communications department was co-operating closely with the personnel side who were volunteered by Bryan Wilson, NFC's personnel director, to arrange the complex presentations at all the various branches and, in some cases, to undertake the actual presentations.

It would be interesting to know Bryan Wilson's popularity rating inside his division at that stage, since the intensive series of presentations were to involve some managers and personnel directors in as many as 60 to 70 presentations in different locations and at all times of the day and night during the first two weeks in August, lugging video machines and 22-inch TV sets from location to location. ('You try getting that lot in the back of a Cortina', was one remark.) But, more seriously, the crash programme could never have been achieved had it not been for the enthusiasm and effort involved on the part of managers in all the companies – most of whom were themselves already sold on the consortium idea.

The 20-minute video programme was completed in remarkably quick time – and it was also remarkably good (it subsequently won a prize in a national video competition). It fell into four main sections: an informal statement by Peter Thompson outlining the opportunities and risks at stake; an explanation of shareholding; an outline of how the buy-out would work; and a brief summary of the make-up of the NFC itself.

Communication has to be a two-way thing, and the Consor-

National Carriers employees at one of NFC's 700-plus locations watching the first video presentation.

tium needed to know the reaction to its efforts. Presenters therefore were armed with questionnaires which they were asked to fill in after making their presentations. Much to everyone's relief the response was gratifyingly positive both in terms of the degree of understanding shown, and the amount of interest generated.

The commitment of top level managers had been assured in the Spring when they had been addressed by Peter Thompson and his team and they too had been invited to fill in questionnaires. Their reaction indicated that the Consortium could count on almost £1 million from that senior echelon in addition to the £250,000 committed by the Consortium itself. The second major 'communication point' had come with the distribution of a printed notice of the buy-out proposals to reach all employees before they finished work on June 18 – the day of the Government announcement and NFC's first Press conference held in the City and organised largely by Universal McCann director Paddy Manning.

The next stage was the briefing of the NFC's 2,300 managers at six meetings held around the country, and addressed by Peter Thompson, James Watson, Philip Mayo and Geoff Pygall – at that time Pickfords Group managing director. At these meetings, as with the initial one for senior managers, an informal poll of support was taken. Thus everyone had a varying degree of knowledge and commitment before the video was produced.

At around this time confidentiality began to impinge on the freedom of action in communication. Everyone from Peter Thompson down had to be careful to say nothing that could be construed as a forecast or as an attempt to indulge in 'share pushing'. There is a fine but extremely important distinction between expressing personal optimism and inviting others to share it, and trying to persuade people that they should buy shares or giving away confidential information. A new phrase was coined within NFC to describe these restrictions: 'the Government Wealth Warning'.

As a back-up to the video and face-to-face meetings the communications department began to put out a series of progress reports, and further information was given in management bulletins and some staff newspapers. These were to become increasingly important in keeping interest alive as initial enthusiasm began to wane somewhat when the overoptimistic timetable began to slip back because of delays in getting through the legal undergrowth and thus completing the Prospectus.

The first of these progress reports went out in July 1981, and concentrated on the initial enthusiastic reaction to the Consortium's ideas both from the workforce and from the media. (On page three there was a montage of Press cuttings which included an intriguing headline from no less than the *Financial Times*: 'Kitson backs National Freight Plan', and quoting Mr Kitson to that effect. A few days later the Transport and General Workers' Union, of which Mr Kitson is deputy general secretary, came out with firm opposition to the plan, a stance it was to maintain right to the bitter end.)

Progress report No. 2 was issued in September 1981 and concentrated on two things: the front and back pages dealt with questions raised by employees concerning the buy-out while the centre pages concentrated on reinforcing the idea of NFC as a single group rather than a collection of unrelated subsidiary companies. This appeared under the banner headline 'NFC: What are we? Vast and varied!' The very first employee question printed in the news-sheet gave an indication of the unease that was beginning to be felt at the delays which were occurring in the buy-out programme as compared with the original timetable:

'I understand that there is some delay in the buy-out programme. Is this because there is doubt about the Government's willingness to accept the NFC's offer, or about the extent of staff support?'

In a sense this was just the sort of question that NFC did not want to gain wide currency since it represented a generally growing feeling, but at least it gave the opportunity for a thoroughly reassuring answer – although this, putting back the probable date for the Prospectus to early November, was still to prove too optimistic. To back the progress reports up NFC prepared a 16-page booklet 'Buying our own company' which was sent to all employees and pensioners (after detailed clearance by the Department of Trade). With a foreword from Peter Thompson, this was designed partly to revive interest by reminding people that everything was still going ahead and partly as an aid to help people understand the Prospectus when it was issued. It also provided a useful trial run for the distribution of the Prospectus, using pensioner mailing lists and employee name and branch address labels produced from the computerised payroll by the NFC's Freight Computer Services company, and involving a massive sorting job by the communications department.

While this booklet was being produced came the all-important Progress Report No. 3, which really did have some progress to report! It announced the signing of the conditional agreement between the Government and NFC for the sale of the company to the Consortium for £53.5 million together with the Government's pledge to use more than £47 million of this money to fund NFC's pension fund deficiencies.

NFC milked this occasion for all the publicity it could. Around 100 slightly mystified senior managers were summoned to Bedford on Saturday October 17, ostensibly to hear about the two alternative buy-out solutions potentially available to the Consortium – depending on the outcome of the 1981 Companies Act: at this stage it was still not clear whether the Consortium would get its 'preferred solution' or would have to settle for the 'ring fence' solution. On this occasion Sir Peter Baldwin, Permanent Secretary to the Department of Transport, co-operated enthusiastically in a bit of dramatic stage management. In front of an audience quite unaware of what was about to happen, he timed his entrance perfectly to coincide with the end of Peter Thompson's address, and the two men calmly proceeded to initial the conditional purchase agreement between the Government and the Consortium. The impact on the managers present was everything that anyone could have desired.

Two days later, on the Monday, there was a Press conference in London to report the signing, which attracted massive favourable coverage including a *Times* leader which began,

> The sale of the National Freight Corporation is not the most important bit of the Government's privatisation package, but it is the most interesting, and the bit that can be welcomed with fewest misgivings.

The headline was 'The workers have it'.

But although progress report No. 3 was trumpeting success it had to explain to the workforce that there were still two possible final solutions, and convince them that it was worth a little patience to go for the better solution which, if it could be achieved, would take a little longer than the less attractive alternative.

With the Prospectus now well advanced a second video was prepared, to be shown after the Prospectus had been distributed, in the same manner as the first, but this time with managers encouraging families and pensioners to attend the showing. This video was designed to help people understand the Prospectus and the form-filling exercises required to buy shares, and again the communications department prepared a comprehensive set of briefing notes for the presenters.

On this occasion a different video technique was employed. One of the advantages of the video route is the sense of familiarity it brings because of its resemblance to watching TV at home, and to enhance this effect one of Britain's most relaxed and best known TV presenters, Frank Bough, was brought in

James Watson, NFC finance director, explaining the Prospectus to a group of employees.

so that the video took the form of a dialogue between himself and Peter Thompson. All this was designed to put what seemed to be a formidable document into a much more relaxed perspective.

But perhaps the most imaginative stroke of all was the use of the freephone facility at the **BRS** Control Centre in Birmingham – normally used for emergency breakdown calls from drivers covered by the **BRS** Rescue scheme – for two weekend phone-ins. For the two weekends that the offer to subscribe for shares was open, the switchboard was manned by NFC directors ready to answer any questions from the worried or confused.

The *coup de grâce* as far as the buy-out communications effort was concerned was delivered in the form of a £53.5 million

Brian Hayward, managing director of National Carriers at the time of the buy-out, and Philip Mayo, NFC director of legal services, doing their bit on the two weekend free phone-ins to answer employee questions about the Prospectus. Mr Hayward is wearing the earphones.

cheque by Peter Thompson to David Howell at the NFC's Fashionflow depot in Camden on February 22 1982, to which drivers from each of NFC's Groups had brought a representative vehicle. In front of a large audience of Press, TV and employees the Secretary of State in turn handed over the National Freight Company share certificate. The money had been raised, and the buy-out was completed.

That was not the end of the communications story of course. From that day on, NFC p.l.c. had a dual communications task: with its workforce, and with more than 10,000 shareholders.

13

HOW THE STAFF REACTED

Q. (SM). What would your reaction have been right at the beginning if your husband had come home from work one night and said he wanted to take out a second mortgage on the house to buy shares in his own company?

A. (Manager's wife). Oh, but we did take out a second mortgage. It was my idea.

> From a conversation at an NFC
> shareholders meeting.

To persuade a third of your staff to invest in a unique experiment, the concept of which was entirely foreign to them, is a remarkable achievement of which NFC is justifiably proud. But every coin has two sides – and if a third of NFC's employees invested it means that two-thirds did not. Applications for shares on Dealing Days by workers who did not subscribe initially show that some of them now wish that they had, but the figures show the proportion to be not very high, and the most likely motivation is the visibly successful performance of the shares in terms of dividends declared and increasing capital value since the offer. It is interesting to note, too, that on Dealing Days there is an overwhelming preponderance of those who took up shares initially wanting to add to their holding. The obvious question is: why the split?

The feedback from the managers and directors who did the visual presentations is interesting, which is not surprising considering the amazing variety of groups of people they could be talking to in any one day, starting perhaps with a breakfast meeting of office workers and traffic management staffs, meeting other groups of different types of workers during the day, and ending up in the small hours of the morning, addressing night shift workshop staff. However this feedback hardly counts as a rigorous statistical analysis.

Certain very broad patterns emerge and they are much as one would expect: where relationships with local management were particularly good and/or where local managers worked hardest to lay the groundwork, attendances tended to be better and the audience more interested and sympathetic; where there was strong union pressure, and particularly where there was a hefty concentration of TGWU membership attendances tended to be more sparse, and the questioning more hostile.

But the general impression one gets is that no real statistical pattern did emerge, and even at different meetings on the same day in roughly the same geographical area, a presenter had no idea of the sort of reception he was going to get. There is one rather nice story of a presenter who went solemnly through the whole video and attendant presentation for the benefit of the sole employee who had turned up. (This happened on another, quite separate occasion when a strong NFC team headed by Sir Robert Lawrence turned up at the House of Commons to brief a Labour Party Committee on the complexities of the pension situation at a time when the Transport Bill was at the Committee stage. On that occasion, only the Chairman of the committee turned up, causing a certain amount of embarrassment all round.)

It is not easy to establish the reasons why so many people opted for staying out of the buy-out scheme: partly because it is almost impossible to ask them. Secrecy surrounding shareholding was something which had to be guaranteed by the Consortium so that there could be no future charges levelled against senior management of discrimination between shareholder members and non-shareholder members, and it is a fact that in some locations shareholder members keep the fact of their shareholding very much to themselves for fear of discrimination or even some form of retaliation from those militantly opposed to the idea of share participation.

Having said this, the most likely reason for non-participation is simply apathy. Throughout the vast majority of British industry the workforce is concerned with what affects them directly – wage levels, overtime rates, bonuses, hours worked and conditions of working. Perhaps the best example of this is the relative lack of concern about the high level of unemployment which exists in Britain: there is no hard evidence that real concern spreads much further down the trade union line than the leadership, where it is used more as a political plank than anything else, except of course in cases where people feel that their own jobs are threatened.

There is firm evidence that the NFC communications programme swayed a large number of people who were initially unenthusiastic, partly by getting across successfully the idea of NFC as an entity, and partly because of the clear way in which the concept, its objectives and the alternatives were spelt out. But experience in other parts of industry show that a large proportion of the workforce, at least in the current climate of thinking, is just not interested in participation through shareholding. The best example of this is Imperial Chemical Industries, one of Britain's biggest industrial companies, which makes a share issue to its workforce every autumn. With monotonous regularity every year, the bulk of these shares find their way into the stock market almost immediately: the great majority of the workforce would rather have money now than a long term interest in the future of the company.

Two other factors certainly had an influence on those who actively decided not to invest, and they are probably interrelated. Undoubtedly many confirmed trade unionists were dissuaded by the lukewarm reception or outright rejection of the idea by their respective unions, while others of the workforce hold a genuine, ingrained, ideological objection to the whole principle of shareholder ownershp.

But while it has not been possible to pinpoint accurately the attitudes and reasons of the non-investors, it was possible to do a survey of the attitudes of those who decided in the end to invest, and to ask them, on a sample basis, about their initial reactions, their decisions to invest, and their views on subsequent developments. This was achieved in such a way as to guarantee their anonymity.

The Consortium has readily adopted standard practice on matters of security when it comes to shareholder privacy and the sanctity of restricted information. For example, when the Prospectus video was being shown, the organisers had strict instructions to ensure that only those who had seen or were entitled to see the Prospectus were admitted to the presentation. As for shareholders, they are known to their employers only if they choose to stand up and identify themselves as such – and all transactions involving shareholders' names are handled at arm's length either by the Shareholders Trust in the matter of share transactions, or by the Registrars – Lloyds Bank, whose Registrars' department is situated in Sussex.

However, using one of the NFC computers, and with the co-operation of the Registrars a means was devised to achieve a simple arms-length survey. The computer was programmed to make a random selection from a list of numbers fed into it and the whole NFC shareholders list was then fed through by number. The computer selected 150 numbers from the list which were then sent to the Registrars who in turn converted the numbers into names and sent off a simple questionnaire with a reply-paid envelope addressed to me personally at my home address.

My questionnaire was restricted to six simple questions:

i. What was your first reaction on hearing about the proposal to buy NFC from the Government? Were you enthusiastic or not? In either case can you say why?

ii. Did you find subsequent information from management helpful? (If yes: how? If no: why?)

iii. What finally decided you to buy shares?

iv. Have you noticed any change of attitudes since you and your colleagues became owners of the company?

v. Are you happy with NFC's progress since you became one of its owners? Can you give reasons for saying yes or no?

The sixth question was designed to try and identify the spread of respondents by company, area, position held and number of shares owned to help evaluate the information given in response to the other five.

Almost one-third of the people asked filled in replies, and although a sample of 50 out of 16,000 plus may not seem a good statistical basis for analysis it compares favourably to the size of sample used by professional polling companies when they try to predict, for example, consumer views on future prosperity.

Also the sample proved to be truly random, with the replies coming from no less than 24 different locations round the country, and the respondents ranging from an apprentice fitter to a couple of people in and around the top echelon of management at Bedford. The only apparent anomaly was that there was no response from Scotland: since the computer's selection was truly random it is statistically possible that none of the questionnaires was sent to Scotland (in the same way that it is possible for ERNIE to pick the same Premium Bond number twice in a row), or it may have been, with Christmas coming up, that my compatriots found better uses for a spare second class stamp.

The results of my questionnaires proved fascinating. It would be reasonable to assume that those most committed to their shareholdings would be the most likely to take time out to reply, but no less than 40 per cent of the respondents said that, for one reason or another, they were not particularly enthusiastic at the start. Here are just some of the reasons they gave:

On hearing about the proposals I was quite shocked and not very enthusiastic as I thought that with our depot losing considerable amounts of money it would be closed at the earliest opportunity. [This is a rather unusual case, since of all the respondents, this person was the only one who was made redundant. As we shall see, job security figured prominently in a number of people's thinking – Author.]

Not enthusiastic as Government was only deserting a sinking ship.

Very interested but rather undecided because of the enormous cost involved, and I believe that 'one man one job' workers getting involved in management just could not work.

No. At first I was a bit dubious because the part of NFC I work for was in a poor trading position. Our charges for carriage were too high, (and I still think they are too high) and we were losing out to competitors.

I was not initially enthusiastic as I would not normally invest in the stock market.

Interested – but not enthusiastic as I was aware of the liability of the pension funds in the operating companies. But it appeared that private groups were more successful in terms of return on capital employed than the State-run NFC so things could only get better.

I did not think it would get enough support.

No. I didn't know the details and opportunities available to me at that stage, I just thought it was another scheme to get some of my money.

My immediate reaction was that my colleagues at 'Branch level' would not benefit and that only the 'upper management' would get any benefit. Consequently I did not give it another thought.

These examples are chosen because they seem to represent a fair cross section of initial objections or uncertainties ranging from job fear, ignorance, suspicion, and some examples of basic financial analysis. Other people expressed similar types of reaction, and in a number of cases which are classed as 'enthusiastic' it is clear that that decision was only reached after considerable family consultation – usually between husband and wife. The quote at the beginning of the chapter is one example of that, and another conversation with a shareholder's wife left the impression that the distaff side of the family was, at least in some grades, a positive influence towards shareholding rather than a negative one. The quote from the wife of a clerical employee is illuminating:

The Consortium rules meant that I could become a shareholder too, and this gives you an involvement in your husband's business that you never had before. I used to get fed up sitting at home all day and then he comes in from work, drops his briefcase and then starts moaning about a terrible day at the office. Now I can share, and take an interest in what's going on. I mean, I've never been to a shareholders meeting in my life before now.

Other wives in the group who were part of the conversation nodded their heads in firm agreement.

But returning to the initial non-enthusiasts who eventually did decide to buy shares, something like three-quarters were favourably impressed by information and explanations given out by management via video presentations and the Progress Reports put out by the communications department, although not all of these people put this down as the major determining factor in their decision to buy shares. Again, it is interesting to note that the relatively small proportion of people who were not originally enthusiastic and who did not find management communication helpful were actively hostile to it. Perhaps the best balanced reply from this small group was

> I accept that management tried to be helpful, but after years of reorganisation and cutbacks I, and other employees of National Carriers saw no sign of improvement and had good reason to be suspicious of management motives.

Another, somewhat ambivalent, reply came from an assistant branch manager who ended up with 100 shares:

> I did find it (management information) useful, but when the people talking to you are in a position to invest £6,000 or more they are bound to sound pretty convincing.

Just for the record, the most hostile reply of the lot was: You *never* find *any* information from management helpful! Since this was the 'sinking ship' chap from question i, the answer to why he decided to buy shares was obviously of considerable interest. The cryptic answer, 'tax relief' was none too illuminating.

Final reasons for buying shares were not too dissimilar between those who were initially unenthusiastic and those who were for the project from the word go. High on the list were job security, the availability of an interest free loan, a desire to be part of the company one worked for, and the lead given by the Consortium and the banks in terms of what they were prepared to commit to the project. Inevitably there were a number of self-confessed gamblers who looked on it rather as they would a punt on the 2.30 at Ascot, but, most surprisingly of all, only eight respondents gave financial gain as a reason for buying shares, and for some of these it was not by any means their first priority.

The response to the survey included a number of replies from pensioners or their next of kin. Here, sentimental involvement and loyalty played a significant part together with a vehemently held view that private enterprise was a better solution than State control – at least two of the pensioners admitted to working in the transport industry before the Second World War. One widow of a deceased former NFC employee gave simply gratitude and a belief in free enterprise as her reason for buying shares, and appreciates the contact maintained by virtue of her receiving all the literature sent to shareholders.

The same lady, although housebound herself, was very much in favour of the regular shareholders meetings which are organised: 'I think they are a thoroughly good idea!' Another widow filled in the form in just two lines: 'I thought I ought to invest in a company which pays me a pension'. On the back of the form was a little addendum: 'My husband worked for NFC for 27 years before he died. He earned the pension for me'.

The reaction of pensioners is included not just to give them an honourable mention but because, in terms of numbers (although not in terms of proportion of shares held) they represent more than 13 per cent of total NFC shareholders. Adding their reasons for buying shares to those given by the workforce and their families, it illustrates a point that is often forgotten in the tight, money-orientated community of the City – that financial gain is not the be-all and end-all in the complex process that leads people towards an investment decision, whether that decision is positive or negative.

Another interesting pointer given by my small survey was the fact that the attempts at financial analysis of the prospectus were by no means confined to accountancy and clerical grade replies. Indeed those who confessed to a gambling streak seemed to have studied the NFC 'form' with a degree of care normally reserved for *The Sporting Life*.

The last two questions on the questionnaire overlap slightly with Chapter 15 which deals with the progress of the Consortium since the buy-out. They are included here however since they are privately given answers to specific questions, and allow a degree of continuity to the answers to the questionnaire as a whole.

The two questions related to changes of attitude, and degree of satisfaction with progress since the Consortium assumed control in February 1982. Around one third of respondents expressed some concern in answer to either or both questions, but perhaps the most interesting factor was that, of these, the split between people who had originally been enthusiastic about buy-out and those who had been unenthusiastic was a dead heat. Again there was no noticeable grouping either by region or by type of job or level within the organisation.

The clearest picture to emerge was that NFC had not been entirely successful in getting across the implications of being a shareholder and the difference between that and being a member of a genuine co-operative. (This was a message that was to show through from time to time at shareholders' meetings as well, with questions from the floor dealing with individual day-to-day grievances relating to their own working problems, competitive position etc., rather than the shape, direction and control of NFC p.l.c. As far as shareholders' meetings are concerned, however, it would be wrong to place too much emphasis on this aspect: it happens in other long-standing public companies, and particularly in the retail trade where no meeting is complete without small shareholders getting up to gripe about the quality of a particular piece of merchandise, or the poor service in one particular store on one particular day.)

To be fair, it would have been a miracle if the Consortium had been able to educate a 25,000 workforce from nationalised industry status to the full implications of being a company owned by its shareholders (albeit these shareholders were all part of the NFC family). But just a couple of quotes will illustrate the ground that has to be made up.

You keep hearing the word participation, but I am afraid that I participate more in the village football club, or garden association. Here you don't get to know what's going off.

I do not think we are informed enough at local level of our depot operations. Our opinions are never asked of. We are still treated as employees and not as part-owners.

Another recurring theme, already mentioned elsewhere in the book, is concern about the amount of NFC's profit which is generated from property sales. In spite of the perfectly justifiable reasons NFC has put forward for treating property profits in this way, shareholders are not alone in their misgivings on this point. A few City eyebrows have been raised a millimetre or so at NFC's decision to put all its property profit through the profit and loss account.

Apart from these recurring themes there is no really obvious pattern of replies – except for a general welcome for the financial results since the shares had already had an upward revaluation by the time the questionnaire was circulated. Some people felt that top management were getting to grips with the problems with a greater sense of urgency, but that there were no signs of any real effects at grass roots level, while others felt that there was a real effect on the shop floor, but no real impact visible at top management level. Significantly, it did not work out that the bottom was blaming the top or *vice versa*.

But perhaps the most remarkable thing of all is noticeable by its absence. In not one letter in reply to the questionnaire, and in not one of many, many conversations over a number of months has any reference been made to the fact that the less profitable divisions are obviously affecting the overall profitability of the group. Those working in the still troubled areas of parcels have referred to the low morale that inevitably accompanies retrenchment and redundancies. But if anything the feeling here has been along the positive lines of, 'if we can make improvements within these areas, how much scope is there for an overall improvement within the rest of the group for everybody's benefits'. Not one person outside the divisions where productivity has been below par for the group has shown any sign of resentment: quibbles appear to be restricted to local areas where, for example, by some quirk BRS and National Carriers have found themselves competing against each other for the same contract, and on differing terms. That may not necessarily be the sort of subject appropriate to shareholder discussion in front of main Board directors, but at least it ensures that such anomalies reach main Board level first hand, and can be pursued from the top if it is felt necessary.

Seasoned shareholders are used to the concept of a group diversified across industries or even with a wide spread of interests within a single industry, since diversification can even out peaks and troughs in overall group performance. It is surprising however that NFC shareholders have so quickly accepted this swings and roundabouts principle.

As a light-hearted postscript to this chapter, thanks to the shareholder who instead of replying to the questionnaire sent a photostat copperplate Christmas greeting from Mr and Mrs Thatcher from No. 10 Downing Street. N.B. for next year: there is only one 'n' in Denis.

14

THE CRITICAL
FORTNIGHT: THE OFFER

It has been a damned serious business. . . . It has been a
damned nice thing – the nearest run thing you ever saw in
your life . . . By God.

> Arthur Wellesley, Duke of Wellington, after
> the Battle of Waterloo. (The more popular,
> but less accurate quote is: 'it was a damn
> close-run thing.')

Leaving aside the military aspect there are certain similarities,
however unlikely it may seem, between Wellington's Waterloo
and the NFC Consortium's share subscription offer. Both
ultimately ended up with resounding victories, but in each case
the outcome was in doubt almost right up to the very last
moment.

The application lists for the 'A' Ordinary shares in the
Consortium opened at 10 a.m. on January 25 1982, and closed
at 3 p.m. on February 16, and the Consortium directors and
their advisers had every apparent cause to be optimistic of the
outcome: as part of the deal the Consortium leaders were
committed to putting in £250,000, somewhere between 100 and
160 senior managers had indicated that they would come up

with another £1 million, and the less senior managers who attended the regional presentations given by Consortium directors had generally given the impression that they would match their enthusiasm with money as far as their means would allow. Reaction from the rest of the workforce had seemed favourable enough to meet the minimum commitment at the very least, particularly with the added incentive of the interest-free Employee Loan Scheme, and the attractive loan terms available from some of the clearing banks. With no quotation in prospect the offer was insulated from any last-minute stock market fluctuations, so what could go wrong?

In the end of course nothing did, but that is going back to the old business of looking unconcernedly at a minefield once you have navigated it safely. Right up until the last few days very few people showed any inclination to navigate it at all. The course that the rate of subscriptions took is dramatically illustrated by the daily graph charted by Philip Mayo throughout the offer period. As can be seen virtually no applications were received until the last few days prior to the offer being closed: it could of course have been extended, but that is usually done only when acceptances are just a whisker short of the required number, and for most of the period it was not just the whiskers that were missing, it was the whole cat.

It was an intensely frustrating period for the Consortium directors. For nearly three years they had been grappling with the prospect of NFC being privatised, and for more than a year they had devoted themselves wholeheartedly to promoting their own buy-out solution. Apart from being at the end of a telephone for the weekend phone-ins they were reduced to sitting back and waiting: you cannot give a share offer for shares the same last-minute advertising boost as a Debenhams sale.

Had it been a normal Offer for Sale through the stock market there would not have been so much at stake. That type of offer is underwritten by City institutions for a small fee so that if the offerors miscalculate the terms of the offer and it is not a success

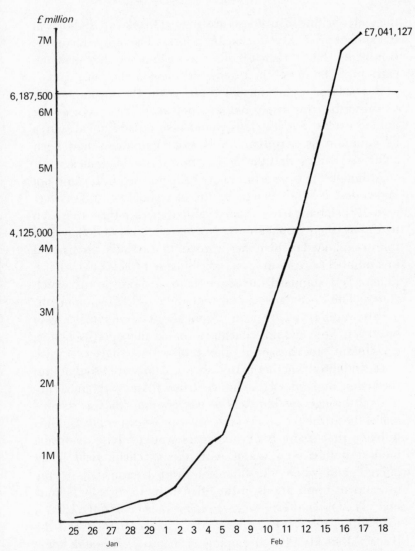

The day-by-day level of applications shows clearly the slow start and the last-minute rush to buy shares. Only four days before the offer closed, the Consortium still had not received the minimum number of applications required in terms of total shares applied for (4.125 million). But in the end it was oversubscribed by about £800,000.

the underwriting institutions are obliged to take up the stock at the agreed price even if it means a loss. (The other side of the coin being that in the case of a successful issue they make an extra profit on top of their underwriting commission.)

But because of the unusual nature of the Consortium's offer to subscribe, this safety net was not available except to the limited extent that Barclays would take up additional shares if minimum subscription levels from employees had been achieved. Failing that the Consortium was a dead duck.

Although the Consortium may have guessed it, it could not know that NFC's novices in the shareholding stakes were actually behaving like seasoned campaigners in their approach to timing their applications. No matter how well they had things explained to them they wanted time to think, discuss and in a number of cases at least, take outside professional advice. (There is a standard introduction to any prospectus which states: 'This document is important and requires your immediate attention. If you are in any doubt about the action, if any, to be taken you should consult a bank manager, solicitor, accountant, stockbroker or other professional adviser.')

It is doubtful whether many stockbrokers were brought into the action, and indeed the chance to buy shares without having to deal through stockbrokers or pay commission was seen as one of the attractive points of the offer by some people. But it is unlikely that many bank managers would advise against a modest purchase of shares with the excellent yield being offered, and where the financial Press commented on the investment implications of the offer, it was generally favourable. The *Financial Times*, *Investors Chronicle*, *Financial Weekly*, not to mention the *Glasgow Herald*, the *Birmingham Post* and the *Western Mail* all advised employees to buy – although some suggested that they should not go as far as the directors who were mortgaging their houses to apply for as many shares as possible.

But there was a period of five weeks between the publication of the prospectus and the first closing date of the offer, and from the end result it is clear that virtually all those who finally bought shares were aware that there was no real time pressure since the shares were not going to be allotted on a first come, first served basis.

The two obvious topics for discussion up to and during the offer period were whether and how much? On the first point, although individuals may have kept their final decision to themselves, it was clearly a major talking point at the group's 700-plus locations. Because of the close working relationships between wages grade employees and local managers the former were often not averse to asking the latter for their advice. As one manager commented:

> My lads came to ask me whether it was a good idea or not. All I could really say was that I thought so, and anyway that I intended to back it. Mind you I was asking my own boss the very same questions and I suppose it went on like that right the way up the line, (pause) . . . I wonder who Peter Thompson asked?

There was obviously a good deal of discussion on the shop floor as well. As one warehouseman remarked in a broad Yorkshire accent (although he doesn't work in Yorkshire) 'There's nowt so queer as folk.' He had announced his intention of buying shares early on, and took a certain amount of ragging from his mates as being 'daft'. Then: 'Later on I discovered that after discussing it amongst themselves they had decided to get on the bandwagon. They'd obviously forgotten what I'd said earlier: they kept telling me what a good idea it was, and how I should follow their example.'

Whether on the floor of the Stock Exchange or the floor of a maintenance depot there is often a roller coaster effect when people congregate. A person might shy at the prospect of entering into a new venture on his own, but he feels happier making that decision if Jack and Jim and Fred are all toying with the idea as well. Wandering round the crowd at the

AGM, where a good deal of mutual congratulation was going on at having made the right decision, I heard a number of snatches of conversation along the lines of, 'mind you I wasn't so sure at the start, but me and the lads talked it over and thought it was worth a go.'

The whether having been decided, the problem came down to how much? Peter Thompson and his colleagues had trodden a very careful path between committing themselves to the hilt in order to emphasise their faith in the project, while at the same time cautioning others not to get in too deep and over-commit themselves. In many cases the interest-free loan had quite a bearing on the whether ('it would have been madness not to take advantage of that', was a fairly common comment) and for many people it put a floor to the how much.

But the fact that it was only a floor is clearly indicated by the average shareholding after the offer was complete – which was £700 per employee after the offers had been scaled down to allow for the over-subscription that finally resulted. (Understandably the average holding among pensioners was lower than that.) Given that there were some substantial holdings of up to 40,000 shares the real staff buy-out element had an average holding of less than £700, but still well above the £200 interest-free loan level. And in spite of all the cautions handed out, people have told me that some of their colleagues 'punted pretty heavily'.

The how much element was probably the most difficult to resolve for people in junior and middle management grades. As careers men they had to pre-suppose a rising real income pattern over time, and work on the assumption that the business under new management (of which they were, after all, a part) would be successful. That being the case the shares would also be a success and there would be little chance of adding significantly to their original holding in the foreseeable future: this was not an American style-share option scheme where option entitlement rose in line with promotion. Against that the average manager in this bracket would typically have a

The rush at Lloyds Registrars as share applications started to flood in.

high mortgage commitment, young children, and could not rule out altogether the possibility that things could just go wrong.

But by February 16 1982 all office and family consultations were over and done with, decisions made, and subscriptions received. In the final few days the applications had flooded in to turn the tide just as dramatically as the tide of battle had turned for the Duke of Wellington. The offer was oversubscribed to the tune of 800,000 shares and applications were scaled down pro rata across the board to take this into account. The legal completion of the sale of National Freight Company to National Freight Consortium p.l.c. took place on February 19 in BMB's offices in the City, and was publicly sealed on February 22 at a ceremony in one of NFC's London depots when Peter Thompson handed David Howell a cheque for '£53,500,000 only' and received the NFC share certificate in exchange. From there on and into the future they really were, to use their own slogan, 'in the driving seat'.

From the left, Sir Robert Lawrence, Lord Camoys of Barclays Merchant Bank, Secretary of State for Transport, David Howell and Mr Peter Thompson, celebrating the successful completion of the buy-out.

15

THE PROGRESS
OF NFC p.l.c.

There are about 1,450 people in this room: another 200 next
door in the cinema and people are still coming in. There is a
real 'family feeling' atmosphere.

> Remark from Peter Thompson, Chairman of
> National Freight Consortium p.l.c. just
> before he formally convened the Company's
> first Annual General Meeting.

Companies, barring accidents, go on forever: books do not. So
what better point to end this part of NFC's story than with the
high-spot of NFC p.l.c.'s short history: its first Annual General
Meeting held at the Hotel Metropole in Birmingham's
National Exhibition Centre on Saturday February 5 1983.

It was indeed a most remarkable occasion. In the year since
the Consortium had bought NFC out of the hands of the
Government it had prospered, and shareholders turned out in
force to celebrate the fact. Birmingham was chosen as the venue
as the most central spot to suit as many as possible of NFC's
far-flung employee shareholders, and a Saturday morning had
been chosen purposely to enable as many people as possible to
attend – transport is not a nine-to-five, five day a week business.

The Consortium had done its best to make it easy for people to get along to the meeting. It had provided coaches and buses to bring people from areas ranging from the south-west to the north-east and beyond, and hundreds more shareholders had made their own way by car, train and mini-van. NFC was not the only group using the Exhibition Centre that day, but for a while one could have been forgiven for thinking so.

The official attendance figure given out was 'over 1,700 NFC shareholders', based on the number of registration cards filled in – some of them photostated because the original supply proved inadequate. But the total number of people present was certainly in excess of that: some people had made a family outing of the occasion. The Metropole's huge conference room was packed, as was the cinema used for the overflow of people

A point from the floor from one of the 1,700-plus shareholders in the Consortium who attended the first annual general meeting in Birmingham.

still arriving, and even then it became a case of standing room only at the back. In spite of the best efforts of the organisers in estimating the likely turnout they had underestimated substantially – and only just got away with it.

In seventeen years of attending AGMs and EGMs I have never seen anything like it. Even the bitterest takeover battles had not attracted that sort of turnout, and my more senior colleagues can remember few occasions when there were bigger attendances, which have occurred with about the same frequency as a heatwave in December. On those rare occasions the companies involved had massive numbers of shareholders: around 16 per cent of NFC's shareholders turned up at Birmingham; if that proportion of Marks and Spencer shareholders turned up for a single meeting Wembley Stadium would be a more appropriate venue. In short, it was the most extraordinary Annual General Meeting I have ever attended. The Press table too was overflowing, and BBC TV was up against competition from French and German TV stations for the best vantage points.

As AGMs go there was an unusual air of informality, although care was taken to make sure that all the legal requirements were fulfilled. The simple fact was that to something like 95 per cent of the people packed into the Metropole they were fulfilling a totally new role. I do not know how many hundreds of meetings I have covered over the years, but it was certainly the first time I have ever heard the representative of the group auditors clapped for doing his statutory duty of reading out the report of the auditors to the assembled meeting. (No-one seemed quite sure of the protocol so to be on the safe side everyone was clapped.)

But for all the good humour and family feeling the meeting was an important one, and an agenda of 25 resolutions had to be completed before anyone could think of a break for lunch. The majority of the resolutions were simply a formality, but there were a couple of items that gave rise to a certain amount of controversy, and NFC's newly fledged shareholders showed no hesitation in exercising their right of questioning and criticism.

The first item on the agenda, normal to all public companies and rarely any problem, is to adopt the report and accounts which had been sent to shareholders some time in advance of the meeting. Except in the case of the dividend it is not easy to measure what improvement the Consortium achieved in its first eight months trading since there are no comparable figures for the previous year, and anyway the picture is further clouded by property sales and other extraordinary items. However, the tone of the report left shareholders in little doubt that things were improving. In his Chairman's Statement Mr Thompson reported a profit of £10 million before dividends, tax and extraordinary items, and went on to say:

> This result can be regarded as an encouraging start to the Consortium's life, bearing in mind that during the whole period the economy was flat and the transport industry, in which we primarily operate, was still suffering from fierce competition and overcapacity. It is early days yet but the rate of trading profit is higher than last year and has been improving over the period.

Recognising the disquiet over the fact that so much of the Consortium's profits were derived from the sale of property rather than through trading Mr Thompson pointed out that trading profit was sufficient to cover both interest payments and the dividend without recourse to property profits (although the picture looks rather different if extraordinary items are taken into account).

The three other main points covered in the report were a higher than forecast dividend, the company plans on debt reduction and new initiatives on the negotiation and structure of wages and the introduction of bonus incentives for clerical staff for the first time.

The improvement in the dividend was a handsome one. The

prospectus had forecast a net dividend (that is after standard rate income tax had been deducted) of 7.5p per share from February to the end of the financial year on October 2. In the event two interim dividends of 4.5p net were declared, with a proposed final of 3p making 12p in all for the eight-month period. Even after taking off income tax that represented a net rate of 18p on an annualised base – more than adequate to cover the interest on any sensible borrowing to invest in the Consortium.

Another tangible bull point (that is to say favourable point) was the group's stated determination to start to reduce its debt burden as quickly as possible. Under the agreement with the banks no repayments were due until February 1984. However, even before the annual general meeting the Consortium had already paid off a first tranche of £6 million, and further reduction in debt was earmarked as a high priority for the financial year 1983/4. The proceeds of property realisation and sale were earmarked for this purpose, indicating that while profit on the sale of property would still be shown as normal profit in the profit and loss account, much of the actual cash realised would be used to reduce indebtedness.

The changes in employee relations allied to the setting up of a small committee to review overall organisation under the chairmanship of Peter Thompson himself was a foretaste of the speed at which Mr Thompson wanted to move the group firmly and finally into the private sector way of thinking. All these factors, taken with the upward revaluation of the shares from £1 to £2 over the period resulted in an enthusiastic reception of the Report and Accounts.

Apart from a number of resolutions there were two bones of contention, both of which related to the shareholding structure. There was some considerable discontent expressed about the order of priorities being followed by the Share Trust, and a number of employee shareholders were also suspicious of the proposed increase in capital and one-for-one scrip issue.

The fact of the matter is that no broody hen could be more

protective about a new born chick than founder-shareholders are in jealously guarding the shares which they bought when they first came on offer. Some months before the AGM I was introduced to a gentleman described in the friendliest way as a shop steward who delighted in giving the management hell at every possible opportunity. The prospect of a chat with this bluff, outspoken chap offered the possibility of getting a view (possibly extreme?) that might differ markedly from the views expressed by directors, endless financial and technical advisers, and even other shareholders who had little direct interest in union affairs.

What, I asked tentatively, was his general view of the buy-out? (It had already taken place and friend shop-steward had taken up shares.) 'Best bloody thing that ever happened to NFC', was the terse reply. 'Has it', I enquired, 'altered views within the group?' 'Of course it has. Before it was the traditional "them and us". Now we all have a common interest. The lads know they are working for themselves and not just an anonymous company. Now we identify with the NFC and not just the company we work for.'

But what about the people who did not apply for shares initially? Shouldn't they be allowed to buy shares now so that more of the lads know that they are working for themselves? 'Not bloody likely', came the explosive reply. 'Not even at £2 a share [the then striking price]. We took the risk – and it was a risk – therefore we should get the reward. Every new employee should be allowed the opportunity to buy shares – that's only fair. But not people who had the opportunity first time round and didn't take it.'

It was not long before I discovered that a good number of other shareholders felt the same way inclined, although they expressed it less vehemently, and sure enough it came over loud and clear at the AGM. It started when Mr Victor Paige gave details of Dealing Day number 2 (November 1982). There were 46,000 shares on offer, and applications for 196,000. New employees were given an allocation scaled down on the same basis as the original offer. There was also a small scaling down in applications from existing employees who had not previously applied for shares – collectively they asked for 6,300 shares and received, collectively, just 400 less than that amount. This left just 40,200 shares for existing shareholders who had applied for nearly 173,000. They each got 200 shares plus just 8 per cent of the balance applied for. Not surprisingly, this brought forward a protest that the Consortium's original backers were being relegated to a poor third place.

The same argument – or discussion – carried on into the resolution proposing the one-for-one scrip issue. The main idea of this was to help in the process of widening share ownership among NFC members and the three-pronged case for this was put by Philip Mayo: it would enhance the sense of unity; it would bring greater commitment to improving the business, and it would expand the feeling of part ownership. The fourth prong to the argument, which was left unstated, was of course that the wider the share ownership spread, the more difficult renationalisation would become.

The bonus issue was approved without any difficulty, but not before a variety of ideas was paraded. To quote from NFC's own AGM report:

> The ensuing questions and discussion revealed a strong feeling among shareholders that employees had all had their chances at the original share issue, and there was no case for giving them special treatment now.

One proposal which received considerable approval from the body of the meeting was that future scaling down should be on a straight arithmetical rather than a percentage basis. Both Mr Paige, for the Share Trust, and Mr Thompson as Chairman of the Consortium promised that the various issues raised would be examined. But it seemed a little ironic that Peter Thompson's plans to widen the share ownership base should be challenged by those whose initial support made the deal possible in the first place. Even the Board is not entirely unanimous on the idea that shareholders should take a profit on some of their holding in order to release shares to promote wider ownership, and should NFC continue to progress at anything like its present rate the chances of worker-shareholders being prepared to let in outside shareholders via a stock market quotation some four years ahead look suspiciously close to nil.

In the nature of things it may well be that the situation will sort itself out. So far at least all the Consortium news has been good news, but that for sure cannot go on indefinitely, and a change in circumstances could bring potential buyers and sellers closer to matching. Not yet, however, on the basis of current year information given by Finance Director James Watson to the AGM, and a subsequent announcement from Mr Paige. Mr Watson told the meeting that the current year's trading had got off to a good start, and a continued improvement was expected during the rest of the financial year. He backed this up by declaring an interim dividend of 5p to be paid at the same time as the final dividend for last year, and right at the end of the formal proceedings Mr Paige put the icing on the cake by announcing a new independent value on the shares of £2.45.

Ironically, the more that Mr Thompson and his colleagues manage to keep up this sort of progress, the less anxious will many people be to part company with their shares. The NFC has its shareholders behind it at the moment, virtually to the last man and woman, but it may well be that Mr Thompson will have to give way a little when balancing the views of his original shareholders against any dilution in their equity (for that is what the wider share ownership programme implies and the fact that the total proportion of the equity which would remain within the NFC family would be the same is another consideration altogether) against his own strongly felt desire to further increase the scope of his revolutionary concept.

Nor does the problem exist simply on a one-way basis. On

dealing day 2 only 20 non-shareholders from the existing workforce applied to become shareholders. Therefore even if Mr Thompson does achieve the 'float' of shares required to meet his plans he still has a major exercise to persuade people to take them up. Mr Mayo announced plans for a further substantial public relations push to persuade more people to join in, and said there would be a repeat of the £200 interest-free loan offer for those who accepted. The upper and lower limit for the number of shares available on this second time round offer would be 500 and 50 shares respectively and the cost of mounting the exercise would, according to James Watson, be somewhere in the region of £50,000.

One of the problems about dealing with the 'ifs' about NFC's future is that in its new form it is still a baby, albeit a precocious one. Only time and the experience of different types of trading conditions will form a basis for formulating patterns of behaviour amongst its shareholders. A normal investor with a portfolio of shares would surely be thinking of taking some profit on a holding which had performed as NFC has done. After all, in the space of just about a year, the shares have gone up by 145 per cent and shareholders have received a massive 17 per cent tax-paid yield on their shares.

Even if the company continues to prosper it cannot go on doing so at the same break-neck speed. This is not meant to be any sort of investment projection that the shares have shot their bolt. Indeed, if the signs of recovery in the economy detected by the Confederation of British Industry is not yet another false dawn, then this can only enhance NFC's trading prospects and take it towards achieving Peter Thompson's stated aim of increasing profit from trading in relation to profit from the sale of property assets. But one wonders just how much effect such considerations, both positive and negative, will have on NFC's shareholders. It is hard to forget the low level of priority attached to purely financial considerations when people were considering whether or not to buy shares in the first place.

But Peter Thompson and his colleagues are already looking

further ahead in other directions, and after the formal proceedings of the AGM were concluded Peter Thompson immediately
launched into an informal discussion with shareholders and
announced plans for opinion pollsters MORI to survey shareholder reactions on a whole range of issues. This had its lighter
moments as Mr Peter Hutton of MORI took the floor to explain
the sampling procedures and subsequent weighting techniques
which would be employed to give a true picture. This did not sit
well with some of NFC's hard-headed shareholders, with one
saying bluntly that 'the weighted-average type of survey was a
waste of time and money and was susceptible to manipulation'.
A beleaguered Mr Hutton defended his firm's reputation and
expertise, but indicated a willingness to follow shareholders'
wishes. At this stage Peter Thompson stepped in, perhaps a
little rashly, to ask shareholders if they would *all* like to get
questionnaires. His reward for that enquiry was an overwhelming show of hands in favour of such a proposal. It was hard to
tell for sure under the glare of the spotlights, but the man from
MORI seemed to turn a shade or two paler at this prospect.

It was quite obvious what Mr Thompson had in mind. He
wanted a much clearer picture of what shareholders wanted on
a whole variety of topics that the brash new baby had not yet
had time to consider. He and his Board wanted to know
whether shareholders would like NFC to become a flamboyant
dash for growth company, or whether they would prefer a more
stately 'blue chip' approach to growth; what were their views
on the frequency of dividend payments; did they want direct
shareholder, employee or trade union representation on the
Board? Mr Thompson wanted shareholders' answers to all
these questions, and on the thorny one of wider share
ownership: 'You have given us the tools today for wider share
ownership, but we want your answers to specific questions
before going ahead'.

The shareholders got their wish, and within a few weeks of
the AGM every one received through the post a 32-part
questionnaire from MORI. The answers were being analysed

as this was written but on the immediate matter of widening share ownership there was clear support, with 70 per cent in favour and only 15 per cent against. This attitude gained further support from the perhaps surprising 81 per cent of respondents who claimed to have invested in the first place because they approved of employee share ownership. But although so many supported the idea in theory, when it came to the point only 26 per cent said they were in favour of shareholders actually offering up shares for non-shareholding employees and an even lower number (21 per cent) said they were actually willing to do so themselves.

It is not often one is minded to describe an annual general meeting as a birthday party, but in a way that is just what it was. The trials and tribulations of the past three years were all but forgotten. Shareholders had every right to be pleased at the way things had worked out for them to that point, but before they got to the cakes and ale they were already having their thoughts directed towards future progress and just what form it should take. If NFC's progress is maintained, and share-holders' enthusiasm along with it, then Birmingham's Met-ropole Hotel will just not be big enough to accommodate the guests at NFC's second birthday party in 1984.

16

CONCLUSIONS

Life is the art of drawing sufficient conclusions from
insufficient premisses.

Quote from nineteenth-century writer
Samuel Butler.

This book has been fascinating to write. It is obviously about a
success story, because people are not usually inclined to employ
other people to write 60,000 words about their failures.
Hopefully however, it is objective enough to show not just
where those involved avoided pitfalls, but also to indicate
where they did not spot the hazard, fell right into it, and had to
climb back out again.

From my own point of view, one of the most enjoyable
aspects has been tracing the steps of people who have been
trying (largely successfully) to break new ground. The City of
London is rightly famous for its position as the world's leading
financial centre and its proud boast is its flexibility in meeting
new situations: nevertheless it is encouraging to see that boast
put to the test in most unusual circumstances and pass with
flying colours. The great Nathan Rothschild, founder of the
London branch of the famous Rothschild banking family would
have approved of the willingness of the banks to take real

entrepreneurial risks in backing the Consortium, and their preparedness to back their instincts on people rather than just on columns of figures.

This was the way of things in the late eighteenth and early nineteenth centuries when the great merchant banking houses flourished, and it brings the discussion, perhaps circuitously, right back to the present day and the continuing importance of personalities.

One aspect of the NFC's fortunes over the past three or more years which has not received enough attention in the course of the book was the outstanding contributions made by NFC's very strong team of non-executive directors. In his chairman's statement Peter Thompson pays specific tribute to Sir Robert Lawrence and to the retiring non-executive directors, Peter Scott, Jack Sieve and Peter Spriddell. He could, with equal justification, have included Frank Law, Victor Paige, Sir Ronald Swayne, and Ron Watson of Barclays Bank (the banks' representative on the Board).

To give just two examples: behind a couple of paragraphs in the chapter on pensions was a series of more than 30 unofficial meetings and discussions at top level where Victor Paige played an invaluable part in helping to resolve difficulties and towards achieving the best possible final outcome for NFC's Pensions Funds. Frank Law, who like Sir Robert Lawrence was a 'founder member' of NFC, was constantly active on the political front, often with a behind-the-scenes involvement where quiet chats can help to reach a consensus that might not be possible in formal discussion across the negotiating table.

More generally, the non-executive directors were in a better position than those with executive involvement to test the water of external attitudes: who if any, were potential predators if NFC were to be put up for grabs? Would the object be an arranged marriage – or simple rape? It is not easy for executive directors to put such questions.

At a time when the advisability and worth of non-executive directors is constantly being called into question on the basis of 'it's a sinecure for old chums', the NFC buy-out is an example of the real benefit that can be obtained from the contacts and wealth of experience which older and wiser men can offer. Business at the top level is still a people business, and it does not really matter whether the links are old school tie or Harvard Business School meritocracy, the fact remains. The personal files of NFC directors are sprinkled with correspondence relating to the buy-out with people who had not even the remotest indirect connection with what was going on, but the interchange of ideas, or just thoughts, often led to the exploration of new avenues.

Without the restraining and guiding hand of the non-executive directors as a buffer between the Consortium and the Government on the one hand and the City on the other, it is quite possible that the aggressive enthusiasm of Peter Thompson and his team might have failed to clear all the formidable obstacles in front of them. And often the guiding hand also held an oil can to help the machinery work more smoothly. Of course this way of operating can lead to potential conflict of interest, but in the real world this is usually more potential than apparent, and at this level abusers of such a position are rare.

Another aspect which receives insufficient acknowledgement in the body of the text is luck. NFC has had its fair share of bad luck with timing and market conditions, not to mention the loss of the BREPS contract at a crucial moment going against it. But how many of NFC's shareholders realise that part of the reason for their very happy first trading period can be traced to a Mr Paul Volcker who spends most of his time sitting either behind a desk or attending top-level meetings in Washington D.C. Mr Volcker, as chairman of the Federal Reserve Board, is rather more powerful in the United States than our own Governor of the Bank of England is here (which is saying something), and it is in no small measure due to his impact on the US Administration and the US banking system that US interest rates were kept stable or falling during the period – and with exchange controls no longer in existence UK interest rates cannot stand aloof from movements in US rates. Had interest rates returned to an upward spiral the results of the highly geared consortium could have looked a lot less favourable. In this respect timing, for once, was on NFC's side, and coming back to this side of the Atlantic – referring to the way the buy-out path was smoothed by the 1981 Companies Act it is hard to forget Giles Hopkinson's remark: 'I have never in my whole career known a barrier to fall down so co-incidentally'.

A third conclusion must be that the route followed by NFC, although it might be helpful to others considering a similar exercise, is most unlikely to be tailormade to fit. In a paper written for a conference in Barcelona last March Peter Thompson listed seven factors which he considered an essential background to the success of the NFC Buy-out. In abridged form they are as follows:

i. participative management style
ii. high quality communications
iii. first class consultation machinery with trade unions
iv. profit-orientated remuneration
v. this concept must extend to wage earners to replace quantity-related bonuses
vi. ability to measure profitability in relatively small units
vii. a workforce which, given the opportunity to do so, is prepared to take a share in the business

But perhaps the most compelling conclusion of all is that where there is a will there is usually a way. I have never understood people's aversion to clichés since they convey admirably in shorthand form the sense of what one is trying to say, and two spring immediately to mind. The first is that where there is a will there is a way, and the second, that you make your own luck. Unless it is well hidden Peter Thompson does not have a descendent of Robert the Bruce's spider on the wall of his office (the success of Bruce's spider to spin a thread between two walls at the seventh attempt persuaded Bruce from the depths of gloom to try just once more for the Kingship of Scotland, and on that occasion successfully, so the legend goes) but without Mr Thompson's absolute refusal to be beaten, and without his ability to inspire his colleagues to the same amount of effort as he himself was prepared to put in, there is every possibility that the Consortium would not be the reality that it is today.

The keen-eyed reader may have spotted some apparent inconsistencies in this book. Some may be accidental, but principally they are there for two main reasons. The first is that NFC as a trading group was not in limbo from May 1979 to February 1983. Management, on top of all the privatisation activity, was getting on with the job of rationalising NFC according to plan, and adapting its attitudes to meet changing business circumstances. Therefore the group structure was constantly changing. Over a period of more than three years there were noticeable changes in the number of people employed, the number of operational locations, the number of vehicles, and the makeup of the property portfolio.

The second reason is that the book is as much about people as it is about facts, and many 'facts' are not absolute, but are open to interpretation. Different people see the same situation in different ways, and each person has his own view of the part he or she played in any given event. Also, time is a great distorter, and here access to original files proved a great help in supplementing incomplete recollection of events that had occurred sometimes three years before an interview. Histories that attempt to give a definitive account are always suspect.

NFC shareholders are far from typical of the breed, but their range of reasons for buying shares and their reluctance to part with them is interesting. Only time will tell, but I suspect time will show that it is not simply the excellent financial performance that retains shareholder loyalty. I have seen hundreds of 'small' shareholder portfolios where the shares have been bought in small numbers and once bought never sold: often the reason for the original purchase was not primarily financial anyway.

(This usually leads to a portfolio with far too many different shares bought in dribs and drabs over a period of 30 years or more, and currently not worth very much. But I will never forget a scruffy piece of paper from an elderly lady whose average investment in around 20 shares was less than £100 a time. A few had gone bust, but the rest, taking into account scrip issues and takeover bids turned out to have a current value of around £160,000.)

Coming to NFC's own finances, it would be churlish to criticise a new issue which has performed so well in such a short space of time, but equally it would be wildly optimistic to expect the share price to double every year. So far property has been to NFC what North Sea Oil has been to the economy: it has buoyed profits through a period of depression, and the cash from property sales is strengthening the balance sheet by paying off debt. But as with oil, property provides a breathing space, not a long term solution: only trading can provide that, and that is the real challenge facing the new NFC.

I must stress that these conclusions, although probably generally acceptable, are my own – except those specifically attributable to Peter Thompson. That said, I think that Peter Thompson's vision of spreading a new attitude throughout the whole of NFC's 25,000 workforce is likely to be a longer term exercise than he would like.

But the Consortium is now an established fact, and its performance so far well ahead of even optimistic expectations. Writing the story has been fun, and informative in a number of ways. I hope reading it has the same effects.

Appendix 1

TIMETABLE OF KEY DATES

1948   Post-war Labour Government starts to nationalise British long-distance road haulage; sets up Road Haulage Executive and British Road Services.

1953   Conservative Government starts to return nationalised road haulage to private sector; unsold 'rump' continues as British Road Services.

1962   Transport Holding Company set up by Conservative Government to absorb all state-owned non-rail transport activities including British Road Services.

1968   National Freight Corporation set up to take over (in January 1969) all state-owned road freight including British Rail road fleet, and is given controlling interest in ex-rail

186

1968 – cont.	Freightliners company. NFC gets five-year subsidy to help with losses on ex-rail companies (but only takes it up for three years).
1969–82	NFC reduces staff from 66,000 to 25,000 and vehicles from 34,500 to 16,000 without major industrial relations problems.
1972–73	NFC makes its first small net profits.
1975	NFC in financial difficulties, with £31 million loss for the year. Government appoints consultants to examine the Corporation's finances and makes cash flow grants to support the business.
1976	NFC top management team reorganised. Peter Thompson appointed Deputy Chairman (Operations), and Chief Executive in February 1977.
1977	Conservative Party produces transport policy document, 'The Right Track' pledging the introduction of private capital into NFC.
1978	Labour Government provides

| 1978 – cont. | capital reconstruction for NFC, reducing capital debt by £53 million to £100 million and providing a three-year capital expenditure grant totalling £15 million for National Carriers. Government agrees to reimburse NFC for some inherited pensions and travel costs. Freightliners company returned to BR. |

1979
April

Conservative General Election Manifesto specifically names NFC as candidate for 'privatisation'.

April 27

NFC Board Paper examines possible effects of a Conservative Government on the Corporation.

May

Conservative Government elected.

June 25

J. Henry Schroder Wagg, leading merchant bankers, appointed as financial advisers to NFC.

July

Schroders' report to NFC Board puts tentative valuation of between £57 million and £90 million on NFC.

1979 July – cont. Envisages Offer for Sale in mid-1981.

August 17 Department of Transport asks Schroders to act as joint advisers to Government and NFC as long as no conflict of interest arises. Schroders agrees. Department accepts necessity to fund deficiencies in NFC pension funds before any Offer for Sale possible.

August 22 Department of Transport circulates relevant trades unions with its proposals to sell most or all of NFC to the public.

November 17 Transport Bill published, providing for NFC to become a limited company and giving Minister powers to open it to private investors.

1980
June Transport Act 1980 passed.

June 30 National Freight Company Ltd formally incorporated, with nominal capital of £1,000.

October 1 National Freight Company Ltd replaces National Freight Corporation. £100 million

1980 October 1 – cont.	debt to Government is extinguished and Minister of Transport becomes the shareholder in new company.
End 1980 to early 1981	Consortium idea being conceived.
1981 January 26	Schroders confirms downgrading of NFC profit forecasts and revises Offer for Sale timetable to mid-1982 at the earliest.
February 27	Founder-members of 'Cabal' produce restricted-circulation document 'Principles of a Management-led Buy-out'.
March 10	Consortium solution raised at NFC Chairman's committee meeting.
March 18	Consortium idea raised at full NFC Board meeting. Referred back to Executive Committee for further investigation.
April 9	Sir Robert Lawrence, NFC chairman, raises consortium solution with Norman Fowler, Secretary of State for Transport. Gets encouragement to investigate further.

1981 – cont.

April 14   NFC Board decides that consortium solution is best of the possible alternatives. This decision is subsequently cleared with Schroders and the Department of Transport.

April 24   First NFC meeting with Barclays Merchant Bank, in Gracechurch Street in the City.

April 29   Full-day presentation to Barclays team at NFC's Bedford headquarters.

May 1–22   Barclays evaluates proposition for the Consortium buy-out.

June 5   Barclays says 'yes' in principle to arranging the necessary funds to support the Consortium buy-out solution.

June 9 and 10   Proposals put to senior management in confidence. Enthusiastic response and promise of support.

June–July   Regional presentations to all NFC managers by top team.

June 18   Government announcement of proposed Consortium solution. NFC Press conference, supported by

1981 June 18 – cont.	BMB. All NFC employees notified individually of proposals. Trade unions informed.
July 24	Work starts on Prospectus.
July 30	Two possible solutions emerge. One depends on outcome of 1981 Companies Bill. Second solution possible without Companies Bill, but less favourable to NFC shareholders.
August	Video-supported presentations by managers at over 700 locations to whole NFC workforce.
October 1	Presentation to proposed banking syndicate.
October 15	Barclays Merchant Bank and Schroders (acting for the Government) agree final valuation of price: £53.5 million – with £47.3 million, subject to minor adjustments, to be paid by the Government to fund historic pension fund deficiencies.
October 17	Sir Peter Baldwin and Peter Thompson initial the conditional agreement for purchase of NFC.

1981
    November 25   Agreement on property valuation and validity for security against loans.

    November 27   National Freight Consortium p.l.c. formally incorporated, with authorised capital of £8.5 million.

    December 11–18   Further downgrading of profit forecasts incorporated in Prospectus.

    December 11–18   Loan agreement finalised.

    December 24   Short-term finance package agreed.

1982
    January 15   Prospectus published, inviting subscription for 6,187,500 £1 Ordinary Shares. Net dividend of 7.5p forecast for period from Consortium takeover to October 2 year end.

    January   Second video presentation to whole workforce.

    January 25   Subscription lists opened.

    February 16   Subscription lists closed. Offer oversubscribed by some 800,000 shares. Applications scaled down accordingly.

1982

February 19	Legal completion in London of sale of NFC to National Freight Consortium p.l.c.
February 22	Ceremony attended by staff and press to mark completion of the buy-out. Peter Thompson presents David Howell, Secretary of State for Transport, with cheque for £53.5 million in exchange for NFC share certificate.
June	First independent share valuation at £1.65p a share.
July 1	First interim dividend of 4.5p a share, net.
August 6	First Dealing Day.
October 26	Second interim dividend of 4.5p a share, net.
October	Second independent share valuation at £2 per share.
November 12	Second Dealing Day.

1983

February 5	First AGM of NFC p.l.c. Final dividend of 3p per share, net, making total of 12p against forecast 7.5p. First interim dividend of 5p per share, net, declared for

1983 February 5 – cont.	1982/83 financial year. Proposals of one-for-one bonus issue approved overwhelmingly. Third independent share valuation of £2.45 announced.
March 11	Third Dealing Day.
April	Second interim divident of 5p per share net. Shares revalued at £1.60 per share (equivalent to £3.20).

Appendix 2

ACTIVE SUBSIDIARY AND ASSOCIATED COMPANIES OF THE NFC GROUP AT THE TIME OF THE BUY-OUT IN FEBRUARY 1982

* Employees of companies marked with an asterisk were not eligible to purchase shares in the Consortium

Schedule 1 Active subsidiary companies of NFC

British Road Services Group
  British Road Services Limited
  Eastern British Road Services Limited
  Midlands British Road Services Limited
  Morton's (BRS) Limited
  Norton Eastern British Road Services Limited
  Watsons (Carriers) Limited
  Hanson Haulage Limited
  North Western British Road Services Limited
  Bridges Transport Limited
  William Cooper & Sons (Carriers) Limited
  Southern British Road Services Limited
  H. S. Morgan Transport (Southampton) Limited
  Western British Road Services Limited

National Carriers Group
  National Carriers Limited
  Fashionflow Limited

Pickfords Group
  Pickfords Industrial Limited
  Pickfords Removals Limited
  Pickfords Travel Service Limited
  Howship & Company Limited

Roadline UK Group
  Roadline UK Limited
  Islandlink (Jersey) Limited

Special Traffics Group
  Cartransport Limited
  Containerway and Roadferry Limited
  Ferry Trailers, Limited

  Cotrali-Pickfords Limited
  Vincent-Cottell Limited
  Southampton Border Freight Limited
  *Cotrali SARL
  Lawther and Harvey Limited

  *Lawther and Harvey (Ireland) Limited

  Pickfords International Air Charter Co. Limited
  Summers the Plumbers Limited
  Tankfreight Limited
  Felixstowe Tank Developments Limited
  Waste Management Limited
  Norwaste Limited
  Holiday Moss (Landfill) Limited
  Questquill Limited
  Hedco Landfill Limited
  Freight Computer Services Limited
  K. D. Scott Limited

Scottish Freight Company Limited
  Scottish Parcel Services Limited
  Scottish Road Services Limited

Tempco International Limited
  Tempco TI Heathrow Limited
  Tempco TI Engineering Services Limited
  *Gerdor Limited

Other companies
  NFC International Holdings Limited
  National Freight Company (International) Limited
  *NV Pickfords International S.A.

  *Pickfords International (Nederland) B.V.

  Star Bodies (NFC) Limited

Schedule 2 Subsidiary companies which, although not trading, hold property in their name

Airlink (European) Limited
Caledonian Bulk Liquids Limited
D. McKinnon (Transport) Limited
Eurexpress Modes Limited
Fashionflow (National Carriers) Limited
Harold Wood and Sons Limited
Loadlink Limited
Manchester Number One Bonded Warehouse Company
  Limited
NFC Properties Limited
PBDS (National Carriers) Limited
Pickfords International (UK) Limited
Pickfords Tank Haulage Limited
Scottish Road Services (North) Limited
Scottish Road Services (West) Limited
J. & E. Transport Limited
C. H. Ward & Sons Limited

Schedule 3 Companies supplying services which are also subsidiaries

Freight Indemnity and Guarantee Company Limited
NFC Freight Nominees Limited
NFC Pensions Nominees Limited
NFC Trustees Limited

Schedule 4 Active associated companies of NFC

*C.L. Instruments Limited
*Grainhurst Properties Limited
*Irish Cold Stores Limited

Tempco Severnside Limited
*Kinlochleven Road Transport Company Limited
*Northern Ireland Carriers Limited

*Tidiways Limited

INDEX

References in *italic* refer to illustrations.